WINDJAMMER WATCHING
ON THE COAST OF MAINE

WINDJAMMER WATCHING ON THE COAST OF MAINE

A Guide to the Famous Windjammer Fleet and 34 Other Traditional Sailing Vessels

Virginia L. Thorndike

With Photographs by the Author

Ah, Maine!
Merry Christmas
C.

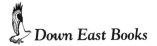

Down East Books

ISBN 0-89272-324-6

Library of Congress Catalog Card Number 92-83835

Cover and text design by Ktaadn Kreations

Printed and bound at Capital City Press, Montpelier, Vt.

2   4   6   8   9   7   5   3   1

Down East Books, P. O. Box 679, Camden, ME 04843

Contents

Foreword

Here on the coast of Maine we have a unique opportunity to enjoy a dwindling resource: large and historic sailing vessels. Not so very long ago there were thousands of working schooners; today there are only a few, but a disproportionate number of them appear here in Maine. We are fortunate to have such a rich variety of vessels come through our waters every year. The old-time coasters, fishing vessels, pilot boats, and yachts that work in the windjammer trade represent only a few of them. Many other vessels, with a variety of histories and missions, live here on the coast or come every summer.

In some circles, "head boats"—those which carry vacationers—are looked down upon, as if taking tourists around were in some way a dishonorable profession. In other circles, the nonprofit vessels are equally disparaged; they are seen to be living a beggar's life. From a strictly pragmatic point of view, I don't care what the ownership or job of a vessel is as long as long as she remains healthy and sailing, where I can enjoy seeing her.

Whatever their missions here, the schooners and other traditional sailing vessels provide pleasure to all who see them, and each has her own interesting story. I hope this field guide will convey both specific information (how to identify individual vessels) and a hint of the rich history that still lives on this coast.

Who's Here

Due to space limitations, the information in this book is limited to those vessels which have some public accessibility. A large number are supporting themselves and their operators by taking people onto the water for day sails, overnight trips, or longer excursions. A variety of schools and training programs operate sailing vessels as part of their curriculum, and some vessels are on civic goodwill missions.

This book centers on the sixteen large vessels home-ported in Penobscot Bay, which continues its tradition as the home of the Maine windjammer fleet; in 1992 fourteen schooners and a ketch sailed from Rockland, Rockport, and Camden. Penobscot Bay is also the home of Maine's official State Sailing Vessel, the *Bowdoin*, which now belongs to the Maine Maritime Academy and hails from Castine. I consider each of these in some detail. Also provided are brief write-ups and photographs of thirty-three other vessels that sail the Maine coast full- or part-time.

There are any number of private vessels out on the bays that are every bit as interesting and beautiful as many listed here, but they are beyond the scope of this guide.

Vessel Specifications

Measurements are given as length on deck, beam, and draft, unless otherwise stated. Displacement is given in long tons (2240 pounds) for the vessel with half load, when both light and loaded figures were known. Some of the older vessels that are "grand-fathered" haven't undergone the measurements the Coast Guard now requires for newer vessels, and their actual displacement is not known.

Terminology

Every subset of sailing people has its own terminology: Gloucester fishermen, Delaware Bay oystermen, coastermen, sailors on full ships, yachting folk, and so on. I have made no attempt to be particularly authentic or consistent to any style; in general,

I have described each vessel in the terms her own captain used, but undoubtedly this effort has not been fully successful. I apologize to anyone I may have inadvertently offended with incorrect nomenclature.

A sketch on page 127 shows the most common names for the most obvious parts of the vessels, and the glossary at the back of the book defines terms that may not be familiar to all.

I'm told it is no longer politically correct to call boats "she." I feel very sad about this, as I think that the appellation is one of respect and admiration for both vessel and gender.

A friend of mine bought a truck that she called Agatha. I remarked that a truck seems a masculine sort of vehicle, but she replied that she hadn't know where to look on a truck to ascertain its sex. I know where to look on a schooner: in the heart.

Following the example of just about everyone involved with the vessels themselves, I shall refer to them as female. Can anything called "it" have a soul?

Acknowledgments

This book would not have been possible without the help of the owners, sailors, and followers of each vessel described. They all were generous with time and photographs, and made the research thoroughly enjoyable.

Most of all I have to thank my husband, Phil Roberts, Jr., who said his name didn't need to appear on the cover page as long as I acknowledged that he did all the work. In spite of my direction, he got me to the right place to photograph each schooner, he was with me on all the face-to-face interviews, and he became as crazed on the subject of schooners as I did. A fellow enthusiast makes all the difference.

Schooners in the Bay

Maine's coast provides extraordinary cruising ground because of both its geography and the sailing company. Anyone spending time on the water between Bar Harbor and Boothbay will see

American Eagle, Roseway, Nathaniel Bowditch,
Spirit of Massachusetts, *and* J. & E. Riggin *at the finish of the*
1991 Great Schooner Race.

schooners. It's hard to make passage through Merchants Row or Eggemoggin Reach without seeing one, and often in Penobscot or Blue Hill bays five or even ten big schooners may be within sight at one time, a reminder of the bygone days of working sail. From land, too, the schooners can be seen, at night anchored quietly in a harbor, or in the daytime, perhaps miles off, their sails bright against the sea or horizon.

The *Bowdoin*, Maine's official sailing vessel, come back to an academic mission, sailing from Maine Maritime Academy at Castine. The windjammer fleet, fifteen large sailing vessels that offer coastal cruises to paying customers, is centered in Rockland, Rockport, and Camden. Schooners also take passengers out for short cruises and day sails from Boothbay, Rockland, Camden, and Bar Harbor. And many other schooners and historic vessels—public, private, and commercial—are coming to be part of this panoply of sail. It seems that nearly every interesting vessel will show up here sooner or later.

Windjammer was once a pejorative term, used at the turn of the century by seamen on steamships to refer to those sailing craft still working. It has more recently been taken on by the cruise operators, who prefer it to the self-explanatory "dude schooner," as the earlier passenger schooners were known. (They also were known as "skinboats," "head boats," and "cattle boats" in the early days of the trade. The worst name, "love barges," came during World War II, when nearly all the passengers were single women.)

The vessels in the windjammer fleet today range in age from more than 120 years to about a decade. The older craft have worked in various capacities in locations all along the Atlantic coast. Some were built as coasting schooners, performing the service that trucks fulfill today, carrying raw material, produce, and supplies from one coastal community to another. Others made ocean passages carrying freight. Some fished for swordfish on the Grand Banks or for mackerel, or for oysters on Delaware Bay, and a couple served as pilot boats, delivering pilots to guide ships into or out of Portland and Boston harbors. A few were originally built as private yachts. Although the Bowdoin is not now part of the windjammer fleet, she was once, and continues to make her home in Penobscot Bay. She was built for scientific exploration and education. Some of the vessels had auxiliary engines when they were built; others did not but were later fitted with engines. Some, while initially designed for sail, worked primarily under power until they were reconverted to join the cruise fleet. A few have never had power, always depending on yawl boats or other external sources when their sails don't carry them where they need to go.

In the mid-1930s sail had all but lost its commercial viability. Schooners still sailed the coast, fishing or carrying cargo and becoming increasingly rough and tattered, but making a living was difficult—and dangerous, due to lack of maintenance, which in turn was caused by the limited financial return. Captain Frank Swift saw a business opportunity in taking passengers out for cruises along the Maine coast on old working schooners. He started slowly in 1936 with a pair of small chartered vessels. But the cruises caught on, and by 1939 he had a passenger waiting list for his three schooners, one of which, the *Mattie* (now called *Grace Bailey*), still carries passengers today.

Captain Swift kept adding to his fleet, and in 1948 had nine vessels operating out of Camden. His schooners were sold or retired one by one over the years, but other captains were joining the trade. Schooners were once cheap and readily available—found resting next to a pier where they happened to land after their last paying trip. By the 1960s most were beyond repair. (Wiscasset's famous hulks, the *Luther Little* and the *Hesper*, are two that weren't rescued. Generations of travelers crossing the Route One bridge have watched them slowly collapse into the tidal flats of the Sheepscot River.)

The *Eva S. Cullison* at wharf, c. 1950.
Penobscot Marine Museum collection, Carroll Thayer Berry photo.

The first vessel built specifically for the Maine cruise business was completed in 1962. The launching of the *Mary Day* signaled a significant change in attitude; "use her up and buy another" was replaced with recognition of the value of preservation. Since then, the *Angelique* and the *Heritage* have been built for the Maine trade. Other new vessels have been built, many of them in Maine even though their primary sailing ground is elsewhere, and efforts are being made countrywide to preserve other old schooners. A number of these have been found, either still working in another capacity or retired but not entirely beyond hope, and with tremendous amounts of work they have been rebuilt.

The older schooners in the Maine windjammer fleet have all

had major repairs if not full rebuilds, as has the *Bowdoin*. It was said before her rebuild that if you left the *Stephen Taber* alone for eight hours she would just gracefully go to bottom. Indeed, on one trip in the 1970s she made a stop at Billings Marine in Stonington so that a day might be spent caulking. Of the six windjammers operating in 1965, five still sail every week: *Grace Bailey* (*Mattie*) and *Mercantile*—both originally in Captain Swift's fleet—*Stephen Taber*, *Victory Chimes*, and *Mary Day*. All but *Mary Day*, a youngster yet, have been rebuilt. The sixth, *Adventure*, has been taken to her old home port of Gloucester, Massachusetts, as a historical exhibit, and repair work is being done on her there.

Major changes have been made in the passenger fleet and its operation since Captain Swift's early days, when no vessel carried a radio or electric power and there were no Coast Guard inspections. Passengers provided their own bedding; men slept on one side of the vessel and women on the other; water was carried on deck, and there were few amenities. On his first passenger trip, made in 1936 in the *Annie Kimball*, Captain Swift made a stop in Rockland to install a head. Even thirteen years later, the only power on one of the Captain Swift's schooners was a ten-horse outboard on a skiff.

Today the Coast Guard inspections are rigorous, safety is a primary concern, and the creature comforts have been improved considerably. Vessels have hot water and showers available, amenities unheard of in coasting days. The flavor of the cruises is very different from the old days, when skippers and their crews were commercial sailors to whom the destination was the goal and the vessel merely the tool to get there. Today the purpose of the trip is the sailing itself, and the vessel is cherished.

The windjammer fleet has been called a floating museum, and so it is, with representatives from a variety of styles and functions

One of the "dude schooner" crews in 1954.
Penobscot Marine Museum collection, Carroll Thayer Berry photo.

of working sailing craft, including two schooners that have supported themselves for more than 120 years, the *Stephen Taber* and
the *Lewis R. French*, the first under sail throughout, the second in
more modern adaptations. But except in the case of the *Bowdoin*,
which continues to sail north into Arctic waters, a cruise today has
few of the hardships of sea life of a century ago. With the days of
working sail it mimics, a windjammer cruise has in common only
the ocean, the hull, and the power of the wind and weather—not
insignificant things to share.

Windjammer People

Every windjammer cruise is different. Some weeks offer clear northwest breezes for days on end, while others seem to have more than their share of fog or rain. Wildlife spottings change from one week to another; more seals or eagles or whales are seen one week and more ospreys or porpoises or loons the next. But the biggest variable is the people, both the passengers and the schooner's own crews.

Whether the windjammer skippers have come to schooners from small boats or from the merchant marine, or just grew up in the business, they all love their work. They would have to or they wouldn't survive. It's an intense job during the season, with no time "off duty." The captain is responsible for the vessel at all times when she's out of port, and in the few hours between each week's landing and the beginning of the next trip, the vessel must be maintained and reprovisioned and all shoreside business must be taken care of.

Of course every captain and crew member loves the sailing. Although the windjammer business is changing, with technology and materials evolving to make the experience safer and more comfortable, the actual sailing hasn't changed a bit in the century or more that some of these schooners have been working. Every skipper takes pride in sailing his vessel to the best of her capability; informal races are common among the schooners, and everyone knows which is the best point of sail or weather condition for each vessel. Both passengers and crew like the competition; the skippers appear nonchalant, but they see everything, and the passengers enjoy the contest. They like learning how to handle the sheets and headsails to get the last bit of speed possible from each moment's changing conditions. And they all enjoy gently rubbing a competitor's nose in his schooner's defeats. One skipper whose vessel goes to windward better than off the wind enjoys quoting Captain Jim Sharp: "Even a bale of hay can go downwind."

Sometimes the competition is a little subtler. When there's no wind on a Monday morning, the Rockland fleet hangs by the breakwater, their sails hanging limp, each skipper hoping someone else will start his motor first. Or on a rainy day or a ferociously windy one, everyone keeps an eye on everyone else; if one puts up sails to move on, the others feel they ought to go, too.

Not all the sailing is fun. There are those rainy, foggy, or "breezy" days, and every skipper has a squall story to tell. But even these stories are told with enthusiasm once the squall itself is history. One captain reports that every skipper has put his schooner aground sometime or another. "How embarrassed you get depends on what the tide happens to be when you do it. I had to do it just after high tide—you don't just kedge off a schooner. But I was lucky; the fog was so thick no one else ever saw it." Another captain doesn't admit to ever having hit the bottom, "but if we haven't been aground it doesn't mean we haven't been embarrassed, breaking something right in front of everyone." And a captain quotes a new skipper some years back who said that each week offered "five and a half days of pleasure and twenty minutes of sheer terror," recognizing that docking one of these large vessels, particularly those with no engine, takes tremendous skill.

The skippers all enjoy being part of the history the windjammer fleet as a whole represents. Each vessel has her own tale to tell, each distinct and interesting in its own right, but when asked which schooner they would choose if they could have any in the fleet, all the skippers chose their own. (A few admitted to a nostalgic affection for the now-retired *Adventure* but still would opt for their own.)

"The passenger trade has kept these boats working in an honest business," says one skipper. "None of us is getting rich, but the schooners are making a living for their owners. No one's giving fundraising dinners to support them, and no one's taking any handouts from the government. It's free enterprise at its best."

The Maine windjammer business has kept alive the knowledge and traditions of sailing and large wooden boat maintenance that would otherwise have gone the way of so many arts, skills, and crafts of the past. The windjammer fleet, dating as it does back to the days of the old coastermen, is a continuum of tradition, today's skippers having learned the trade under sailors who carried cargo in schooners or under men who themselves learned from the old-timers. Most of the captains of traditional sailing vessels throughout the United States have at one time or another worked in the Maine windjammer fleet; it is a *de facto* national training ground for working sailors.

Being a windjammer captain requires knowledge and interest in many fields—sailing and the ocean, and perhaps history and woodworking and esthetics and mechanics—and to make a go of it, a captain must be attentive to the financial aspects of the business. But as important as any of his skills and talents is the enjoyment of people. The passengers are part of nearly every moment of the season, and for many of them, says one skipper, just being aboard an oceangoing vessel is as foreign as being on Apollo 7. The repeat passengers act as an interface between the schooner people and the new passengers, many of whom sit aboard on Sunday night, before the Monday-morning departure, wondering whether this trip was such a good idea. The folks returning for more offer encouragement and they enjoy helping the newcomers figure out how to operate the head or negotiate the companionways.

The hardest thing at first for a lot of passengers, says one skipper, is that there's no schedule. "It takes them a while to understand that we really *don't* have a clue where we'll be anchoring, we're not just saying we don't. You can always say where we are, what direction we're headed, how fast, but not where we'll end up or when." Another captain reports, "They tease you a lot—'You don't have any idea where you're going!'—but they love it." Not having a fixed itinerary, being able to go wherever looks most favorable, is one of the pleasures of the windjammer cruise. "I used to worry a lot about it, where to go," says one captain, "but there's no sense in that, so you just do what you want to do. And that usually is just fine."

Few of the cruises are planned around a particular theme, or if they are, it may be for the enjoyment of the crew as much as for the passengers. In general, the personality of the skipper sets the vessel's tone. Some like to "let it happen," while others take a more guiding role in the activities on board, leading sea chanteys, telling stories, explaining maritime conventions or nomenclature. All welcome questions and end up talking a lot about schooners, the ocean and its wildlife, islands, Maine geology, maritime history, human nature, and the state of the universe.

The hours the ship's company spend together encourage close conversation, and true friendships develop both between passengers and between the schooner's crew and her customers. (How many captains over the years have ended up marrying former passengers? At least one in the current fleet.)

Reading is very common, aloud or otherwise. "One week everybody on board is reading trash," a skipper reports, "and the next, they're all reading classics, three of them *War and Peace*." At the end of a week, while everyone else is scurrying around helping to furl sails and sharing phone numbers and addresses with one another, there's often one person sitting in a corner frantically trying to finish a murder mystery found aboard. "Take it with you," says the captain. "You can send it back." (Usually that same person will have already contributed one or two books to the collection.) One skipper reads E.B. White essays aloud in the evenings, another favors Ruth Moore's ballads of Maine's seafaring people.

Stories and songs—not necessarily about the sea, though many are—are heard on board most of the vessels at one time or another. One captain says he likes to tell down east stories; another says his repeat passengers insist that he retell the Maine tales he was brought up with, whether he wants to or not. They may have heard the stories nineteen times, but they like to see the reactions of the new passengers. A third skipper makes a point of sitting back and listening to his passengers' stories. Working sea chanteys are part of life on one vessel, while the storytelling maritime songs of Gordon Bok and Stan Rogers are common on another.

Passengers create their own themes. Common standing jokes often appear and reappear for the length of the voyage. Sometimes everybody's playing Trivial Pursuit, and other times that would be the last thing anyone would want to do. Sometimes one organizer in the group, given support, can make a unique experience for all: a passenger once instigated an elaborate murder game that continued the whole week, and another schooner's race effort was once supported by a loud cheerleading section led by an enthusiastic passenger.

Sometimes what the captain or a crew member is doing creates a storm of interest—carving or tying knots, for instance. On one cruise everyone was making knotted mats. "One woman never did learn how to do that mat," reported a smiling former captain. "Every morning for six days I showed her, but she never did get it."

A lot of brass gets polished out on the bay, too. The entire ship's company takes pride in the vessel.

Then there are the "schooner junkies" who sail as often as they can. Mattie Mosher started sailing on the cruise schooners in 1940 and says she would rather sail than eat. She met her husband on the *Mattie* (now *Grace Bailey*) in 1946 and has sailed on her every chance she has gotten. She was given her nickname in honor of the schooner, and is known as Mattie to everyone in Maine, where she and her husband moved after his retirement in order to be near the schooners. "Whenever anyone phones and calls me Martha, I know it's someone from New Jersey," she says. Her husband died a few years ago, but the relationships she's developed over the years with other passengers and with the skippers remain important to her, and she sails several weeks each summer. "I'd sail across the ocean in a canoe with Captain Sharp," she says, and even though he is no longer sailing regularly, when he takes a week for one of the other skippers, she's aboard. Her affection for the schooner people is reciprocated; Captain Ray Williamson, when he rebuilt the *Mattie*, put the old name board over Mattie Mosher's bunk. Mrs. Mosher has sailed on several other vessels as well, but it is clear that the *Mattie* is her favorite, even though she's called *Grace Bailey* now. They know each other well after a half century.

There are many happy customers in the windjammer business, and crew members have a good time, too. Nowadays most of them are college students or young people taking time off before college or after graduation. Some are putting in time toward their own captain's licenses and may themselves be skippering a Maine windjammer or another sailing vessel one of these days.

The captains' enthusiasm is the most striking, however. One skipper said that when he bought his vessel he thought he'd be good for fifteen years. He's been sailing her nearly half that time now and still thinks he'd like another fifteen.

Design of Schooners

Note: The diagram on page 127 explains many of the terms used in this chapter.

New England Fishing Vessels

Early New England fishing took place close to shore, and the vessels used were small, many of them pinkies. The *Summertime* and the reproduction *Maine* both show the pinky's distinctive stern design (see pages 118 and 110).

By the middle of the nineteenth century, fishermen were going offshore to the Grand Banks, and larger, stronger, faster vessels were built. The two significant designs remaining today are the *Fredonia* from the 1880s, on whose lines the *Spirit of Massachusetts* (page 118) was built, and the McManus-originated spoon bow of the 1890s which typifies the last Gloucestermen. The latter were fast, seaworthy, and elegant vessels, above and below the water. Their lines are graceful from their long, overhanging bows through their sheerlines to their transom sterns. Heavy, deep keeled, and powerful, they have been cited as the most handsome and functional of sailing vessels.

In the second quarter of the twentieth century, the trend toward engine power was established. The *American Eagle* (1930) was one of the last vessels built that depended largely on sail but carried an auxiliary engine. The *Sherman Zwicker* (1942) was one of the last hybrids built, and used sail only to steady her (page 117).

Pilot Schooners

Even before 1800 schooners were used to put pilots aboard incoming ships to guide them into port. These schooners often represented the latest design theories for fast and seaworthy sailing vessels. Because they stood by in deep water, sometimes for days on end and in all weathers, they were also designed to be comfortable and safe in a seaway. The *Timberwind* was specifically designed as a pilot vessel. She looks much like a Gloucester fisherman, as does the *Roseway*, who served Boston pilots for more than thirty years.

The Timberwind.

Coasting Schooners

Until after the turn of the century, nearly all material that traveled from one part of the Northeastern coast of the United States to another went by schooner. Uncounted schooners were built and launched, mostly for local trips. Although some went to the West Indies, they were not usually intended for deep-water voyages, which remained the job of the square-rigged ships. Both deep- and shallow-draft schooners were designed, and as there was

The Grace Bailey *beached for work on her hull, 1992.*
Their shallow draft and straight keels made it easy to beach
the coasters when necessary.

a practical limit to the size of two-masted schooners, three-, four-, five-, and six-masters, and finally even a seven-master, were constructed. But two-masted, shallow-draft vessels remained the norm for short hauls on the coast of Maine and in Long Island Sound, where their smaller size and shoal draft gave them access to harbors larger vessels couldn't reach. Their long, straight keels allowed them to be beached to load and unload cargo or for repair. They were broad vessels, many with centerboards, and in summer carried topsails on each mast. In the present fleet of windjammers, the *Lewis R. French* and the *Mercantile* from Maine, the *Grace Bailey* and the *Stephen Taber* from New York, and the unusual three-masted *Victory Chimes* from Delaware all originated as coasters.

Delaware Bay Oystermen

Because of the shallowness of the bay waters, the schooners built for oystering on Delaware Bay were constructed in a manner very similar to the bay coasters: shallow drafted and with a long, straight keel. Today's Maine windjammer fleet includes the *Isaac H. Evans* and the *J. & E. Riggin*, which were built for oystering in 1886 and 1927. They are shoal-draft centerboarders that are very similar beneath the waterline to their coasting cousins. The *Riggin's* more recent design is evident in her spoon bow, Gloucesterman look above the water; the *Evans* represents the older style.

Yachts

While sailing for pleasure may have struck the serious merchant sailor or fisherman as foolish, the fact remains that much pleasure has been gained from (and employment given by) the

The Surprise *was originally built as a yacht.*

sport of yachting. Yacht design since the middle of the nineteenth century has been influenced by the desire to go faster than everyone else and by well-intentioned rules meant to even out the competition. These rules have led to extremes in racing yachts, and have not always led to the betterment of their sailors, but throughout the years many cruising yachts have been designed in the fashion of the working vessels of their own or earlier days. In general, yachts were built and finished in a more refined manner than working vessels, and of course they weren't expected to carry massive amounts of cargo. The term *yachty* is used a little derogatorily by some to describe this characteristic. But in some cases it is impossible to designate a particular vessel as a yacht or a working vessel—she may have functioned in both capacities at one time or another. Of the schooners in the Maine windjammer fleet today, *Nathaniel Bowditch*, *Roseway*, and *Wendameen* started life as yachts.

New Construction

The second half of the twentieth century has seen a renewed interest in building traditional schooners. Several are supported by a foundation, city, or nonprofit organization and were built to serve as training or goodwill vessels, *Spirit of Massachusetts* (page 118) and *Pride of Baltimore II* (page 115), for example. Others, such as *Ocean Star* (page 113) and *Bill of Rights* (page 103) belong to profit-making organizations with educational missions. One individual is responsible for the construction of five schooners, all named *Appledore* (pages 100–02), which served a number of functions and now are in the passenger trade under various ownerships. Several vessels have been constructed for and continue to work in the passenger cruise trade; three are in the present Maine windjammer fleet. These have been designed in traditional style, either local (*Mary Day* and *Heritage*) or European (*Angelique*).

Bowdoin
The Maine State Sailing Vessel

The Bowdoin. *Courtesy of the* Bangor Daily News.

Donald B. MacMillan was an explorer and a seaman and a lover of living. In his time he was known to be a leading authority on the Labrador and Greenland coasts, often leading even local fishermen into port through fog and rocky approaches, and much of today's knowledge about that area comes from his work. He was well respected for his achievements, his generosity, and his commitment to learning and education, to his wife, his men, his friends, and the Arctic. His life was in the North, and he shared this life with the *Bowdoin.*

Designed by William Hand to MacMillan's specifications and built at the Hodgdon Brothers yard in East Boothbay in 1921, the Bowdoin is distinct in any fleet of schooners. She was built small, for an exploration vessel, so she could hug the shoreline to avoid heavy ice and in winter be buried in the snow for insulation. She is high in the bow, to work through ice; she has a compact sail rig, being both bald-headed and bowspritless, so as to keep her crew safely aboard in the Arctic seas she sailed; and she carries a barrel on her foremast from which MacMillan himself scouted routes through pack ice. All this can be seen from afar; her overall ruggedness becomes obvious on closer approach, but some of her unique features aren't so apparent. She was designed with two watertight bulkheads so that if her hull were pierced she would remain afloat. (Such bulkheads are required now but were very unusual, if not unheard of, when the *Bowdoin* was built.) Her underbody is deep and narrows as it goes down; pinched by ice, she would pop up and even fall over on her bilges if necessary, righting herself as the ice broke up. Drawing but ten feet, the average Arctic tide, she could be beached at high tide, so her undersides could be worked on, and she'd float herself again as the water returned. She was sheathed in an extra layer of ironwood from the waterline to four feet below, as protection from ice.

The *Bowdoin* has been well tested. On her first trip north, in 1921, she bounced off a solid mass of ice unscathed, and from October of that year until July of 1922 she was iced in while her crew studied terrestrial magnetism and atmospheric electricity. The winter of her second trip she spent 330 days frozen in place at

Refuge Harbor, in northern Greenland, and escaped the following summer only because she was able to break through the ice. In 1929, off Baffin Island, where the tide runs forty-five feet, the *Bowdoin* and the ice mass she was anchored to were suddenly dragged rapidly northward. Mac climbed up to the icebarrel lookout and saw an iceberg the size of a city block sweeping toward them, crushing smaller icepans in its way. He commanded the crew to prepare to abandon ship. (The cook said he was too old to die in

The Bowdoin *at Refuge Harbor, North Greenland, winter 1922–23. Courtesy of Maine Maritime Academy.*

the cold, went below, and, propping his feet up against the stove, smoked a cigarette.) With the engine full ahead, Mac swung the *Bowdoin* back and forth to keep maneuvering room and at the last moment threw her bow hard to port. The berg scraped the starboard rail as it roared by, but the *Bowdoin* suffered no damage.

MacMillan and the *Bowdoin* separated during World War II. The navy sent her north while he worked in Washington, though both were involved in charting Greenland. After the war MacMillan found the *Bowdoin* in Boston Navy Yard—a derelict, stripped, vandalized, and filthy. Then an admiral and more than seventy years old, he worked on her himself all summer. Cummins donated an engine, and the following year the *Bowdoin* and Mac returned to the Arctic.

Mac and the *Bowdoin* made twenty-six voyages north between 1921 and 1954, accompanied after Mac's marriage in the mid-thirties by his wife, Miriam. At one time or another the *Bowdoin* carried scientists of a dozen different disciplines and more than three hundred students (the "Bowdoin boys"), who learned much about the Arctic, life itself, and themselves from her and her skipper.

When Admiral MacMillan retired, the *Bowdoin* was donated to Mystic Seaport, in Mystic, Connecticut, but she wasn't maintained; by 1968 she lay in a back lot under plastic, once again stripped and dying. A group of former "Bowdoin boys" and other enthusiasts formed the Schooner *Bowdoin* Association and brought the vessel to Camden, where Captain Jim Sharp repaired her into sailing condition. He exhibited her and carried passengers and made a trip to Provincetown to allow Admiral MacMillan, then in his nineties, to once again see his vessel under sail.

A 100 percent rebuild was undertaken between 1980 and 1984, spearheaded by John Nugent and supported by many of the "Bowdoin boys" and other contributors. Cummins again donated an engine. Today, the *Bowdoin* is as tough as ever and retains many of the features that MacMillan designed into her. She has been updated in a few areas; she carries the latest electronic gear, and her galley is far more convenient than it was in Mac's day. She still loves a good breeze; on a perfect sailing day it is blowing 30 to 35 knots.

After short stints in a number of programs, including Outward Bound, in 1988 the *Bowdoin* came to Maine Maritime Academy in Castine. Captain Andy Chase, former skipper of the *Westward*, was teaching at the academy and developed a sail training program around the schooner. In 1990 Captain Chase took her back to Labrador, and in 1991 she returned to Greenland. On both trips she revisited many places she had been with MacMillan. The crew met people in remote villages who had known the *Bowdoin* decades before and were both amazed and thrilled to see her again. One octogenarian showed the crew a picture MacMillan took of her when she was twenty-one, and a middle-aged man had a photograph of himself as an infant, given to his mother by the people on the *Bowdoin*. The crew was introduced to sailing conditions totally new to them; uncharted and rocky waters, pack ice, and the complete isolation of Labrador all awed the sailors, if not the schooner.

The *Bowdoin* is now the official Maine State Sailing Vessel, having been granted this honorary title in 1986 by the state legislature and governor. Manned by many crew members who weren't even born when she last was in the North, the *Bowdoin* is returning to her first workplace and being rediscovered by old friends. Through MacMillan the *Bowdoin* made many friends, and she will continue to do so as she goes on with Admiral MacMillan's missions of Arctic exploration and the education of young people.

Bowdoin
length: 88' gross tonnage: 66
beam: 22' sail area: 2,900
draft: 9'6" (full keel) rig: bald-headed knockabout
displacement: 88 tons
power: 190-hp Cummins diesel
no. students: 10 crew: 5

American Eagle

The *American Eagle* is the only true Gloucester fisherman remaining in the windjammer fleet. She was actually built in Gloucester (most hulls were constructed in Essex and fitted out in Gloucester). The *Eagle* wasn't the most refined model of the type, and she was never intended to be a racing schooner. She was a working vessel, and she fished from Gloucester for fifty-three years, decades after the last of the racers were gone.

She was launched in 1930 as the *Andrew and Rosalie*, named for her owner's niece and nephew, whom he adopted after their father died. She was a deep-draft, oceangoing schooner carrying a four-cylinder Cooper Bessemer auxiliary engine. In 1938 the engine was upgraded to a six-cylinder. Like a number of Gloucester fishing vessels during World War II, she was given a patriotic name to balance the fact that many of her crew were probably not American

The American Eagle *during her career as an eastern-rig dragger off Cape Ann, August 1977. Photo by Bill Haynes.*

citizens. A pilothouse was added in 1945, plunked on top of her main cabin. Her stern was chopped off in the fifties after a collision. When it was no longer needed, her bowsprit was sawed off. In 1962 she was made over in the style of a modern eastern-rig dragger: the masts were removed and a Caterpillar engine was installed. Like many a fishing vessel before her, her final job was as a "day boat," taken out only when the weather looked auspicious. A day boat always was in port at night, and maintenance was minimal.

In the late summer of 1983, after more than a half century of fishing, she was laid up. Her present owner, Captain John Foss, bought her about a year later, and although she was able to come to Rockland under her own power, some of her extraneous parts didn't make the whole trip. She arrived at North End Shipyard on Halloween night. She didn't need a costume. "That old slab would make a vulture vomit," said Captain Foss's father-in-law, watching her tie up.

Boots and slickers still hung in the fo'c'sle, left from the twelve-man crews the *American Eagle* had taken to Georges Bank in decades past. Pinholes had corroded all the way through whole stacks of aluminum pots and pans nested in lockers under the leaking decks. The seat lockers in the main cabin were full of gear and parts of engines long gone. The restoration project began with a great many trips to the dump.

Rebuilding took more than a year and was only possible, says Captain Foss, because he and his brother-in-law, Captain Dan Pease, were able to do the work themselves at the North End Shipyard, which Foss owned in partnership with Captains Doug and Linda Lee. Captain Foss estimates that the *American Eagle* was 80 percent original when she was taken up onto the railway. Many of her timbers and planks had to be replaced, not so much because of age as neglect; her deck hadn't been kept tight nor her topsides caulked. She was still about 35 percent original on relaunch. Her stern had returned to an approximation of its original form, and she carried a rig similar to what she had in her youth. She entered the passenger trade in 1986.

The *American Eagle* is fun to sail, according to her skipper. She likes 12 to 20 knots of wind best, though she needn't reef before 25. She's good to windward, able to point higher than many others in the fleet, and her engine, a 190-horse diesel, allows her to go a greater distance from home than some because there's always an easy way back. "You don't have to send the cook down in the yawl boat when the wind dies—you just turn the key." That key sends her along at 8.5 knots, but under sail she can make nearly 13.

Captain Foss enjoys taking *American Eagle* back to Gloucester, which he does each Labor Day weekend for the races there. "We tie up in Gloucester, and she's not our boat any more. She belongs to the fishermen who used to work her." Old men who sailed on her bring their entire families aboard and proudly show them around. The Piscitello brothers, who fished her from the end of World War II until she was laid up, always sail in the race itself, and usually television people come, too. The brothers take over, telling stories and keeping everyone amused. This is just fine with Captain Foss, who is free just to enjoy sailing on his schooner's home grounds.

The rewards of the windjammer business, says Captain Foss, include keeping an old vessel going and proving to the present that the past was a little more sophisticated than we sometimes think. The *American Eagle* is sharing her own history with her guests on every voyage.

American Eagle
length: 92'   gross tonnage: 70
beam: 20'   sail area: 4,600
draft: 11'4" (full keel)
rig: bald-headed; round, tapered masthead
displacement: 107 tons
power: 190-hp diesel

Angelique

The *Angelique* is unique among the Maine windjammers. She is not a schooner at all, and she has a steel hull—although once aboard, it might be hard to realize it, for she has wood throughout. She was designed to resemble a Brixham trawler of the 1890s, the British counterpart of the American Gloucester fisherman. She is distinctive for her plumb bow, big fantail stern, dark sails, and, of course, the gaff topsail ketch rig. She would look at home in the Baltic, where the Maine schooners would look out of place.

Designed by Camden, Maine, artist Imero Gobbato and built in Florida for the Maine trade and possible cruising, the Angelique was finished and fitted out in Maine for the 1981 season. She alone

in the fleet provides an on-deck salon, which gives passengers a comfortable vantage point from which to admire the sea without being out to weather. The cook, who at this writing has been aboard the *Angelique* for six seasons, enjoys the deckhouse too; she says she has the best galley in the fleet, and in fact, the best workplace imaginable. Instead of being enclosed below, the cook's station is forward in the deckhouse with a beautiful view. The *Angelique*'s cookstove runs on kerosene, which is easier on the cook than the woodstoves of most windjammers.

Although the *Angelique* was still very new when Captain Mike McHenry bought her in 1986, he has made a lot of renovations and changes to her that make her feel like his own vessel. He immediately repainted her in more traditional British colors. He has resparred her, still with steel masts and wood tops, gaffs, and booms; he has renovated the cabins and galley; and he put in new plumbing. He has recut the topsails (making five sails that need to be tacked whenever she comes about).

Perhaps the most significant change of all for the person at the helm was the removal of the two big fixed propellers. These were replaced with feathering props. "Now she sails as if someone had taken the emergency brake off." The informal racing among the windjammers is a source of pleasure for most of the skippers, who all know who's good at what and when to stay away so as not to be shown up. "They used to come hunt me down so they could sail by me," Captain McHenry says, but now the *Angelique* is respected as a fast sailer. Of course it helps that Captain McHenry has learned how best to sail the big ketch; he says it's not like sailing a schooner, and not only because at first it was hard for him to remember which was the main and so sent his crew to adjust the wrong sail a few times. Because of her lofty rig, she is particularly strong to windward; when it's blowing her skipper loves to sheet her right in and put her on the wind. He admits she isn't so good downwind, when the schooners' long booms give a big advantage.

The *Angelique* is a strong seagoing vessel, easier to handle offshore than a schooner because of her smaller mainsail. She has a pair of 471 Detroit engines that allow her to venture just a little further than she might otherwise, because if worse comes to worst, she can always come back under power. She likes the wind best between 12 and 15 knots, drops her jib topsail after that, but doesn't need to strike the tops before 20 knots on the wind, more than that off the wind. She's heavy enough that she does need 5 or 6 knots to get going. On the foggiest days, when there's no wind and little prospect of much to come, she chugs easily toward her next anchorage.

Like most of the skippers, Captain McHenry enjoys his passengers. "Windjamming is a form of camping, only you don't have to deal with cooking and ants. The people who come are the kind of people you'd like to have aboard." The *Angelique* carries more passengers than most of the schooners in the fleet, but because of her spaciousness there always is a place to get away from everyone else. Repeat business is the base of any schooner's trade, and the *Angelique* is enjoying more and more repeaters. Great Schooner Race week is made up of some 70 percent repeaters and is always the first week to fill.

The *Angelique* has an entirely different look from the rest of the windjammer fleet, one equally traditional but with a different origin. She has found respect in Maine and in the larger world of sailing and serves her master well.

Angelique

length: 95'   gross tonnage: 99.98
beam: 23'7"   sail area: 5,200
draft: 11'6" (full keel)   rig: gaff topsail ketch, 4 headsails
displacement: 140 tons
power: two 471 Detroit diesels
no. passengers: 31   crew: 5

Grace Bailey

The *Grace Bailey*, although known for fifty years on the coast of Maine as the *Mattie*, was originally named for the builder's daughter. She was built in 1882 on Long Island by sawmill owner Edwin Bailey. The finest materials were available from his yard for her construction, and even though she is said to have been rebuilt in 1906, her present owner says that when he bought her, more than a hundred years after her launching, she was 90 percent original.

The Grace Bailey carried hard pine from Georgia and the

Carolinas to be sawn into wainscoting and other construction materials in New York City, and she made winter trips to the West Indies for fruit. When she was rebuilt or repaired in 1906, she was renamed *Mattie*, after Edwin Bailey's granddaughter, Grace Bailey's niece. In 1914 the *Mattie* moved to New Haven to carry oysters on Long Island Sound.

In 1919 the *Mattie* came to Maine. When Captain H.L. Black, whose vessel had been accidentally rammed by a United States

The Grace Bailey *fully laden. Mystic Seaport Museum photo.*

submarine, was paid by the government for his loss, he bought the *Mattie* and brought her to Bucks Harbor. Captain Black never cashed the government check, though; it was found hidden in the *Mattie*'s master cabin years after he died.

The *Mattie* sailed a few trips to Massachusetts carrying boxboards but more often worked in Penobscot Bay carrying salt, pulpwood, coal, cod, and hardwood (as much as fifty cords at a time). She also took granite from Crotch Island to New York City to be used for the post office and Grand Central Station. She carried a double topsail rig during this period and could move right along.

In 1938 Captain Frank Swift chartered the *Mattie* for his new passenger business. He bought her in 1940, and she has been showing passengers the ocean side of the Maine coast ever since, except briefly during World War II, when she served as a training vessel for Maine Maritime Academy.

She and the *Mercantile* are the last of the schooners from Captain Swift's fleet that are still sailing. During her last decades as the *Mattie*, she was showing her age. Her centerboard trunk leaked so much that it had been sealed up, leaving her to sail without benefit of the board. In recognition of her slowness to come around through the wind, a verse was sung about her:

> *Captain Fred the Mattie obeys,*
> *But she lingers in stays for days and days.*

The *Mattie* sailed under several ownerships and more captains; one, Theodore Schmidt, was aboard during twenty-two years, as passenger, cook, mate, and finally as master. The vessel now belongs to Captain Ray and Ann Williamson, under whose ownership she has been entirely rebuilt. And they have given her back her original name, *Grace Bailey*. The rebuilding was actually a complete restoration of the vessel. The instructions Captain Williamson left for his project manager were simple: put it back the way it was originally. If you take out an oak 9 by 12, put back an oak 9 by 12; if you take out a pine 3 by 3, put back a pine 3 by 3. This order wasn't as easy as it sounds: the *Grace Bailey* is the only member of the fleet constructed with hanging and lodging knees. You don't just walk into your local lumber yard and order one hundred knees! For each and every knee a hackmatack tree had to be found in the woods and cut. But it was important to Captain Williamson to put the *Grace Bailey* back the way she was when first launched, and that's how she is, each gracious detail intact. Her decking is tapered, as are her cabin tops. Her main cabin paneling was taken off piece by piece, each panel marked and then put back when the new structures were in place. To get the old pieces to fit required a complete replication of each angle and curve of the original, no easy feat.

Like many construction jobs, this one took longer than projected. The *Grace Bailey* was relaunched on the last Friday in June 1990. Her first cruise was scheduled for Monday. The mast was stepped on Saturday, fitting-out continued through the weekend, and on Sunday night the passengers arrived and moved into their just-finished cabins. Some thirty hired men were still caulking and rigging, and the passengers joined in and helped. The *Grace Bailey* set sail on Wednesday, July 4, and everyone enjoyed the week.

Captain Williamson wanted to share the old vessel's renewal with someone who knew her and loved her as he did. When he took a week off in the summer of 1991, he asked Captain Schmidt to return and sail as relief skipper. "Don't forget to use the centerboard!" Captain Williamson hollered out as they left. Captain Schmidt says he enjoyed sailing the *Grace Bailey* more than he could have imagined possible. She was fast; she was light on her feet; she tracked straight—the vessel had truly been reborn.

Grace Bailey
length: 80'   gross tonnage: 59
beam: 23'6"   sail area: 3,622
draft: 7' (11'6" board down)
rig: bald-headed; square mastheads
power: yawl boat
no. passengers: 29   crew: 5

Heritage

    The *Heritage* is the youngest of the schooners in the Maine passenger cruise business. Her owners, captains Doug and Linda Lee, with Captain John Foss, started North End Shipyard in Rockland in 1973. They actually reopened an old yard, installing a marine railway to replace the old one that was still there under the mud. As well as doing their own maintenance and schooner reconstructions, they rented out space for others to work on their own projects. By 1979, most of the major work being done to Rockland-based schooners was taking place in the North End Shipyard. Building the *Heritage* was the largest undertaking to date, but she was an exciting and natural next step.

The project was expected to take five years. The Lees sailed the *Isaac H. Evans* and Captain Foss sailed the *Lewis R. French* in the summer, and they all worked on the *Heritage* during the winter.

The Heritage, *transom and yawl boat.*

It seems that the Lees can do whatever they set their minds to; the Heritage is evidence of that. Captain Doug Lee designed her, chose the timber to be used for her significant structures, and, with his wife and partner, constructed the vessel. Any iron parts that were no longer available, mast bands and chainplates and so on, Captain Lee forged himself. A festive launching on April 16, 1983, was attended by a large number of enthusiasts, including representatives of all three major television networks, who happened to be in

Bath for a destroyer launching the day before. The Lees could more than match Bath Iron Works' claim to be on budget and on time, for the *Heritage* was completed not only on budget but also a year ahead of schedule. *Heritage* entered the trade in June 1983.

The *Heritage* was designed in the tradition of the nineteenth-century coaster, with adjustments for comfort but keeping the esthetics of an old vessel. Captain Doug Lee says that she's everything she is supposed to be: big, rugged, comfortable, yet she looks the part. She has a nice motion in a seaway, having the greatest displacement of the coasters in the fleet. She is firm and steady under sail, not the fastest in the fleet, not the slowest. The skippers of other schooners say that in competitive situations Captain Lee knows well how to take tactical advantage of her weight, for example by using her momentum to shoot up to windward toward a competitor, thus forcing the other vessel to tack away.

The *Heritage* has full headroom below decks and other details designed specifically for the passenger trade: her companionway ladders are not ladders at all but stairs (no need to go down backward); she has coach houses over her galley and midships companionways (some of the charm of a historic vessel disappears when you smash your head on a companionway slide that someone has slid shut half-way); a huge skylight brightens the galley, which seats the entire ship's company at one time; heads and generator are housed on deck in the forward deckhouse, where any noise or odor won't bother anyone. Small modifications are made each year to make the vessel easier to run or more comfortable—rounding off a corner of the ice chest, improving the insulation of the chest, adding new snatch blocks to ease raising of the mainsail.

Following the old coaster tradition, the *Heritage* carries a donkey engine, a 1917 one-lunger, which raises the anchor and can be used on the halyards on rainy days when thirty helpers aren't enthusiastic about volunteering. The challenge of sailing such a large vessel without a propelling motor is part of the *Heritage*'s appeal to her skippers. Like her coasting forebears, she carries a yawl boat. She travels 150 to 200 miles a week, and although she doesn't venture beyond Schoodic point the way the powered windjammers sometimes do, her passengers enjoy the unlimited number of little harbors and coves she visits.

A unique feature of the *Heritage*, and indeed perhaps the very reason for her being, is the presence of the Lees' two daughters, Clara and Rachel. The Lee's first vessel, the *Isaac H. Evans*, didn't have room for the girls, who have been a part of the *Heritage*'s crew every summer since they were infants. They operate the yawl boat; the older daughter was going aloft at ten to set the topsail; and either will finish making the sticky buns any time she's asked. That the *Heritage* is a true family endeavor is perhaps her best feature for the Lees and follows the tradition of many Maine coasters before her.

Heritage
length: 94'   gross tonnage: 93
beam: 24'   sail area: 5,200
draft: 8' (18' board down)   rig: main topsail, jib topsail
displacement: 153 tons
power: yawl boat
no. passengers: 33   crew: 8 (plus Clara and Rachel)

Isaac H. Evans

The *Boyd M. Shepard*, as the *Isaac H. Evans* was known originally, was built in Mauricetown, New Jersey, in 1886 to dredge oysters on Delaware Bay. Life expectancy for oyster dredgers at that time was only twenty years, but the Evans family bought her when she was a little over that age and sailed her until 1919, when they rebuilt her and renamed her for their father. She worked until

1933, when the Depression made it no longer economical to fish oysters, and she was beached and sunk with three other draggers in a mud creek. The mud protected her timbers from destruction by freshwater wood-borers. With the return of the oyster market in 1936, she was dug out of the mud, retopped, and put back to

The Isaac H. Evans *in 1942, with a load of oysters.*
Courtesy of Captain Ed Glaser.

dragging. When oystering regulations changed in 1946, permitting full-power dredging, her masts were removed and a pilothouse was added. Twice more she faced extensive repairs—once in 1954 after she was nearly lost during a fire at a gas pier where she was docked, and again in 1966 when ice ripped a plank and sank her. She went back to oystering and remained at that job, an increasingly marginal occupation, until Doug and Linda Lee (now the owners of *Heritage*) bought her in 1971.

The Lees had little money, but they did have ambition, energy, and friends at the Bath Maritime Museum, where they took the *Evans*. Over the course of a couple of years, with the help of a lot of elbow grease (that of both the Lees and volunteers), the *Evans* was returned to her original configuration. She has been sailing in the windjammer fleet since July 1973.

The *Isaac H. Evans* is typical of hundreds of boats built for oystering at the end of the last century and not very different from thousands of coasters, most of them long gone. She has recently been recognized as a Historic Landmark, representing the nineteenth-century Delaware Bay oystermen. Her age is comforting to her present captain, Ed Glaser, who has been her master since 1983. "No matter what I do with her, I'm doing something someone else has done before."

Sailing on the *Evans* gives very much the sense of how a boat was sailed a hundred years ago. Captain Glaser claims there's nothing particularly wonderful about his boat compared with any other in the fleet, but he also says there isn't another boat out there he would rather sail. She's not the fastest in the fleet, but she's especially easy to sail; being deep in the forefoot and wide, she is stable, and she keeps going the way she's pointed. "You can go take a leak and come back and she's still headed where you left her." Guests who come aboard having sailed on smaller craft are surprised by how little attention she requires. But after all, she was built for oystering, not to sail for sport.

Sure, Captain Glaser would like to go as fast as the *Stephen Taber* or the *Lewis R. French*, but he likes to anchor closer to shore than the other fellows do, so he can look for kingfishers through the binoculars, and the *Evans* lets him do that. And she's handy: she backs out of a harbor or does most anything. She's not an offshore boat, Captain Glaser says; she'd make it to England, but he wouldn't have a pleasant trip. She's designed to come home every night. And when she gets to her night anchorage, she behaves herself, just as she does under sail. "She doesn't drag her anchor or do any of those things boats do to people."

The *Isaac H. Evans* has the distinction of being "the boat that sank"—a sudden squall some years back in Eggemoggin Reach swamped her and sent her down—but as Captain Glaser says, she's not the first boat to go down in that location. She is sailing again, which some others can't say, and there are those who believe that a person doesn't really know how to sail until he's had a boat go down with him—"Gives him a little humility." It isn't a bad thing to be reminded of the ocean's power and unpredictability. And the *Evans*, after all, has been down and brought up before. "She's one of the few that's back from the dead."

When Captain Glaser is ashore, he says, he can't sleep at night; he's worrying about this thing and that which need doing. He's fretting, pacing the floor, and making lists. On the *Evans*, he goes to bed at nine or ten and doesn't move till well after sunrise. She'll take care of things.

Isaac H. Evans
length: 65'   gross tonnage: 52
beam: 20'   sail area: 2,600
draft: 6' (14' board down)   rig: main topsail
displacement: 68 tons
power: yawl boat
no. passengers: 22   crew: 4

J. & E. Riggin

The *J. & E. Riggin* is well known on Delaware Bay, and indeed has been recognized by the National Park Service as a Historic Landmark, the best example of the twentieth-century Delaware Bay oyster-dredge boat. She was built by Charles Riggin in Dorchester, New Jersey, in 1927 and named for his two sons, Jake and Ed. All three Riggins captained her at one time or another. She was always known as a light-air vessel, which gave her a major advantage in the short dredging season. She was also known as a fast boat; in 1929 she won the only race ever held in the bay for oystermen and so became for all time the best racer!

The *Riggin* is the subject of many legends among oystermen. One, perhaps not absolutely true, tells of another vessel in the fleet headed in after the day's work, wung out and pushing with her yawl boat and going as fast as she possibly could. Along comes the *Riggin* from behind and right on by, and there's her yawl boat still up in the davits.

The J. & E. Riggin (foreground) with oysters piled on deck,
sailing with three other oystermen in Delaware Bay, around 1930.
Courtesy of Captain Dave and Sue Allen.

In the mid 1940s, when the fishing regulations changed, she was sold by the Riggin family and converted to power. She was taken to Long Island, where for twenty years she fished mackerel and other groundfish. In 1971, still working, she was purchased by a fellow who intended to make her into an operating museum, sailing token cargo around the Cape Cod area. As in so many of these projects, the expense was too much, and the scheme died. In 1974 she was again for sale, and Captain Dave Allen and his wife, Sue, made a quick trip down to Osterville, Massachusetts, hitched a ride out to look her over, chased all around town to find her owner, and agreed to buy her on the spot. They towed her bare hull back to Rockland, where they started rebuilding—a long process, as they were doing the work themselves with the help of a number of volunteers. They did go into it with their eyes open, Captain Allen having been around other rebuilding projects his father and other windjammer owners were involved with, but neither of them was very skilled when they started. They became more so.

Because the New Jersey oystermen were intrigued that the *Riggin* was being rebuilt, the Allens were able to obtain period equipment for her: blocks and davits and ironwork for the mast and other gear. Dick Riggin, the son of Ed Riggin, one of the brothers for whom the *J. & E. Riggin* was named, chased down a lot of equipment for the project, including the vessel's original launching pennant and forty-eight-star American flag.

She was relaunched in 1977 and has been in the Maine windjammer fleet ever since. The trio of the *Riggin*, Dave Allen as master, and Sue Allen as cook have been together the longest of any combination in the fleet. "It's funny," say the Allens. "Now we're among the old guard—we used to be the new kids."

Captain Allen is a second-generation windjammer captain and himself came up through the ranks, as so many have done. His first job was working in the galley of the *Stephen Taber*. (That cook worked many more years on windjammers, but never again hired a male mess hand, he notes.) Sue has been cooking on the schooners for longer than any other cook in the fleet today: seventeen seasons at this writing, fifteen of them on the Riggin. "Really, people come back for the food," says Captain Allen.

Although he says they've been with her so long they take the *Riggin* for granted, Captain Allen admits she's just about right for them. She's a good size, she's fairly stiff, she handles well—"She does what we ask her to do." She's no longer a light-air boat, with the ballast she now carries, but likes 15 or 18 knots of wind best. She's most competitive on the wind, and it pleases her master that she is able to get past some of the other vessels despite being bald-headed. "It's a joy to sail her," he reports. And every year she takes him to some little anchorage he's never been to before.

The *J. & E. Riggin* has the spoon bow and graceful sheer of a Gloucester fisherman, as did many of the later oyster schooners on Delaware Bay. Under the water, however, she has the shallow draft and centerboard of her predecessors, like the coasters. Her rig has been changed since she worked in Delaware Bay; then her masts raked more, she had a single headsail, and her main peaked a little more. Now her sail plan looks more like that of a Maine vessel. She is black, as she has been for nearly all of her life, with a single quiet red stripe. The Allens have recently removed a second, yellow, stripe. They like her clean lines and shy away from anything flashy. She's flashy enough in her own right.

J. & E. Riggin
length: 89'   gross tonnage: 61
beam: 22'6"   sail area: 3,500
draft: 7' (12' board down)   rig: bald-headed
displacement: 75 tons
power: yawl boat
no. passengers: 26   crew: 5

Lewis R. French

Three sons of a storekeeper named Lewis R. French built a coasting schooner in Christmas Cove, South Bristol, Maine, in 1871. They had an unwritten agreement with their father that he would help the project financially. When approached by one or another of his boys, he would say "I'll get to it. I'll get to it," but family history says he never did. By naming the vessel the *Lewis R. French* his sons had the last laugh, if little else; tradition says that when a vessel is named for a living person, that person supplies her with a set of flags. And Mr. French did his duty.

Back in the nineteenth century, as today, regulations were more demanding for vessels over sixty-five feet. The *French* was designed to sneak under that limit. Unlike the other coasters in the windjammer fleet, she has a fixed keel, although she draws little more than most of the centerboarders. Not having a centerboard is good for the accommodations below, which don't have to be constructed around a centerboard trunk.

The Lewis R. French *in Northeast Harbor, about 1900. Courtesy of Captain Dan Pease.*

The *French* has worked along the Maine coast continuously since she was launched. And of the thousands built during the nineteenth century, the *French* is now the only surviving fixed-keel coaster. She is also the only surviving nineteenth-century coaster built in Maine. Some purists discount her because she was converted to power, but because her owners kept up with changing times she was able to support herself commercially for over a hundred years. She carried general freight until 1877, worked as a seiner out of Boothbay for four years, and then returned to coastal trade. A gasoline explosion aboard tore her up in the 1920s, when she apparently had already been modernized to the extent of carrying an engine along with her sails. She was rebuilt powered, with a single spar and a big wheelhouse aft. After a few years carrying lumber and coal, with Vinalhaven as home port, she was taken down east, where she worked for the sardine canneries in Eastport and Lubec. She was still carrying cannery supplies 101 years after her launching.

It is not unusual for someone to come up to the *French* at the dock in Rockland, stand looking at her awhile, peering this way and that, and then tell how he (or his father or his uncle) used to work on her. "I sure did hate loading boxes under that low deck!" said one old fellow wistfully.

Captain John Foss (now of *American Eagle*) found the *Lewis R. French* in Eastport in 1972 and brought her to Rockland for repairs. Even though she had still been working, she was in bad shape. Some of her planking fell right off as they reefed caulking out of the seams. Captain Foss and Doug and Linda Lee (*Heritage*) rebuilt her, returning her rig as close as they could to how it was in her youth. Captain Foss sailed her from 1976 until 1986, when Captain Dan Pease, who had crewed on her for several years, took her over. The purists can be happy today; she carries a yawl boat and has no engine aboard.

The *French* is a good sailer. Captain Pease says she goes as far as any other windjammer, and her shallow draft lets him get places some others can't. He enjoys beating through Eggemoggin Reach with one of the deeper vessels and being able to take half as many tacks, cutting buoys and going closer to shore than they dare. She likes a 15- to 20-knot breeze the best, carrying all her canvas. Her topsails allow her to do well in light airs too. "She's pretty slippery," says Captain Pease.

The *French* has shown her ability to get through the water in recent Great Schooner Races, held each year around the Fourth of July. She has repeat passengers each year who take the race very seriously. They prepare all week, insisting on a few tacks to windward in order to practice bringing the topsail about. Since the *French*'s coaster class starts with the captains ashore, rowing to their vessels at the gun, a lot of work goes into boat retrieval. During practice one year, an enthusiast fell into the water. (In the race itself, everyone managed to stay aboard.) One stalwart passenger took it upon himself to hand hold the staysail club in order to maximize the sail shape in the light airs of 1991's race. A bit of dinghy-racing technique paid off for the *French* in that race; even a vessel with a weight of fifty-six tons can be influenced by the placement of her people. Captain Pease said the idea came from a passenger, but he was pleased that he was able to sneak by a competitor after the passengers all moved to leeward, helping the sails to remain filled. Clearly the *Lewis R. French* and her master like to be fast.

Lewis R. French
length: 64'   gross tonnage: 50
beam: 19'   sail area: 2,900
draft: 7'6"   (fixed keel)   rig: main topsail, jib topsail
displacement: 56 tons
power: yawl boat
no. passengers: 23   crew: 4

Mary Day

    The *Mary Day* was the first vessel built specifically for the Maine windjammer trade. She reflects Captain Havilah ("Buds") Hawkins's lifelong love for both coasting schooners and inventive boat building. It seems inevitable that after stints in the cruise business with two other schooners Captain Hawkins should have turned his hand to designing his own schooner—and that she should be different from all those before her. The *Mary Day* was built in 1962 by Harvey Gamage, of South Bristol, Maine. Gamage had been building schooners and fishing draggers since World War I and went on to build other large sailing vessels after the *Mary Day*, including *Shenandoah*, *Clearwater*, *Bill of Rights*, and *Harvey Gamage*. The *Mary Day* was named for Captain Hawkins's wife, a member of the well-known boatbuilding family from Sedgwick.

The *Mary Day*'s lines are traditional, but she is built for her present job, with a little more refinement than many of the old tough coasters and a lot more comfort. She is relatively high-sided in order to provide headroom below. She has opening windows and skylights in the passenger cabins, providing light and airiness not available in the working coaster of the nineteenth and early twentieth centuries. Her main cabin is large enough to seat all the passengers at once for meals at tables grouped around a Franklin fireplace. She has welcoming companionway stairs in place of the traditional ladders. Her cabin sides slant at a comfortable angle for her passengers sitting on deck to lean against.

Some of the changes to the traditional coaster Captain Hawkins made when he built the *Mary Day* are strictly for his and her own benefit, affecting the passengers not at all. He was tired of replacing rotted timbers in his older coasters, so he left the *Mary Day* ceilingless. He felt that constant exposure to the air would make her framing last better. Thirty years later, he appears to have been right; all her framing is solid, and all is original. He fiberglassed her cabin tops, preventing leakage. Her timbers aren't as heavy as they would have needed to be if she were to carry stone or be loaded to the rails with other heavy cargo, so the vessel's displacement is considerably less than other schooners of her length. Her centerboard is hung in an innovative manner that makes it easier to remove and replace.

The *Mary Day* was known in her early days as "the music boat." She carries a Blake five-stop pedal parlor organ, built in Union, Maine, probably over a hundred years ago. Under Captain Hawkins, an important criterion in crew selection was musical ability. Gordon Bok and many other singers and instrument-players worked on her in her early days, attracted to her and hired because of their musicianship. Dances were held aboard; there is room on deck aft for a full square!

The present organ is the second the *Mary Day* has had; her first burned the year the television version of *Captains Courageous* was filmed in Camden. The film crew simulated a big storm during one dramatic night scene being filmed on *Adventure*, across the harbor from the *Mary Day*. Someone admired how they'd even made the *Mary Day* look as if she were on fire—only that wasn't part of the script; *Mary Day* was indeed afire. Attributed to the spontaneous combustion of turpentine rags, the fire destroyed much of the after section below, including two cabins and the organ. Two weeks' work had her ready for the season as usual, however, though the sculpting of the fire can still be seen beneath the paint above the table.

Captain Hawkins sailed the *Mary Day*, painted white, for twenty years, then turned her over to his son Haddie for five years, during which time she sported black paint. A manx cat named Stump lived aboard then, and surprised more than one passenger as he appeared in their cabins from the bilges in the middle of the night. Since 1988 Captain Steve Cobb and his wife, Chris, have owned the *Mary Day*, the cat has retired to crawl through the undersides of his land-based home, and the *Mary Day* has been painted a very light gray.

The *Mary Day* is the only schooner with double topsail rig in the windjammer fleet. Informal racing among the schooners keeps the captains' enthusiasm high, and Captain Cobb has pride in his vessel's speed. The *Mary Day* is accepted as one of the faster members of the fleet, particularly in light air. Because her topsails come in at 12 knots and she gets reefed at 20, the heavier vessels have an advantage in a strong breeze, and some of the other schooners are more competitive to windward, but Captain Cobb says that off the wind, in 15 knots or less, there's not a member of the fleet that can pass the *Mary Day*.

Mary Day

length: 90'   gross tonnage: 86
beam: 23'6"   sail area: 4,500
draft: 7' (15' board dn)
rig: main and fore topsails; jib topsail
displacement: 90 tons
power: yawl boat
no. passengers: 28   crew: 5

Mercantile

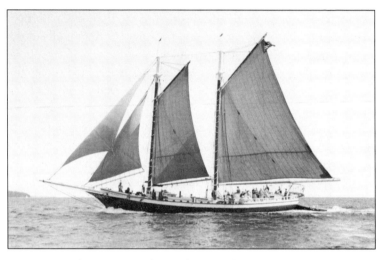

During the winters when other employment wasn't available, the Billings family of Deer Isle built themselves schooners. Around World War I they built five coastermen altogether for various members of the family. It took more than one winter to finish the *Mercantile*, even with three generations of the family involved in the project. The lumber was sawn on site by a wind-powered saw. They used some unorthodox construction techniques, too. Some of the timbers used for her frames still had limbs on them, and as the frame was hewn out, any protruding limbs were simply cut off so they would butt up against the next frame. The *Mercantile* was launched in 1916, and although like most of the coasters she was built with a short life expectancy, she was well (if crudely) con-structed, for here she is today. One of the last sailing vessels built for cargo, she has sailed continuously for nearly eighty years.

The *Mercantile* carried many different cargoes during nearly three decades as a Maine coasting schooner under three of the Billings brothers in succession. Her regular cargo was barrel staves and firewood to the lime kilns along the coast, but each fall after

The Mercantile *sailing wing-and-wing. This 1992 photo shows her with her sheer restored after a major rebuilding in 1989.*

the fishing season she made a number of trips from Swans Island and Frenchboro to Gloucester carrying salt fish and bringing salt back for preserving the next year's catch. She carried several other cargoes as well—lumber, coal, boxwood, and bricks—before trucks took over this job. She is said to have made one trip carrying the most dangerous cargo: unslaked lime. (More than one schooner caught fire from the intense heat of the chemical reaction caused by sea water leaking into their cargoes of unslaked lime.) One night in 1939, while carrying a load of wood, she collided with a steamer on the Penobscot River and suffered considerable damage, but she was taken to Bucksport, unloaded, and repaired and put back in service.

The *Mercantile* left Maine and the Billings family early in World War II, when she was sold and taken to Rhode Island to fish mackerel, but two years later she came back to Maine when Captain Frank Swift bought her for his growing passenger trade. She has been in the cruise business ever since, under four owners and many different skippers.

After three decades in the passenger trade, the *Mercantile* was showing her age. A ditty was sung around the bay:

> *There's so much hog in the* Mercantile,
> *They're serving pork at every meal*

Captain Les Bex raised the *Mercantile*'s stern in 1976, improving her looks and strength, and in 1989 she was fully rebuilt by her current owner, Captain Ray Williamson. By careful planning of space—rearranging cabin walls and berths and making minor adjustments to deckhouses—Captain Williamson increased the *Mercantile*'s passenger capacity by three. At the same time he made her more comfortable, adding a third head and a shower and increasing the galley size so all the passengers can sit down to eat together. He also took the water storage from on deck and put it below, increasing the stability of the vessel, and installed holding tanks for sewage. Even from a distance, the change in the *Mercantile* after her rebuild is obvious; today her sheer is very graceful.

In the summer of 1991, the Billings family held a reunion aboard the *Mercantile*. As an eleven-year-old boy, Captain Bob Billings had worked on the construction of the vessel, at sixteen he had served as a deckhand, and eventually he skippered her himself.

Captain Billings and twenty-eight of his descendents came aboard for a sail, anchoring the first night in Eggemoggin Reach off the beach where she was launched seventy-five years before. He took the wheel again during this trip, passing under the Deer Isle bridge (which hadn't been built when they first sailed the Reach) into view of a huge banner: WELCOME HOME, CAPTAIN BOB AND THE BILLINGS CREW!

The *Mercantile* is listed on the Register of Historic Places, and has also been named a National Landmark. These honors certainly recognize her national historic significance, but as important to the folks who care about her is her local history. The *Mercantile* was constructed within her present cruising ground, with much local material. Into the 1980s she still carried three blocks manufactured at the Knox Mill, which stood on the site of the Camden town pier, where she has berthed for decades. She has spent most of her life right where she is today; she knows every little harbor from the days she carried cargo around the local bays. An old fellow in Frenchboro has greeted her more than once, telling her skipper how he remembers the *Mercantile* coming in for pulpwood and pointing out the wharf where she used to tie up. The *Mercantile* is a living example of coastal Maine history, and she continues to support herself and her owners as she has done for over seventy-five years.

Mercantile

length: 80'   gross tonnage: 47
beam: 22'   sail area: 3,015
draft: 6'7"   (10'7" board down)
rig: bald-headed; square mastheads
power: yawl boat
no. passengers: 29   crew: 5

Nathaniel Bowditch

Both designed by William Hand, the *Nathaniel Bowditch* and the *Bowdoin* were also both built by Hodgdon Brothers in East Boothbay, Maine, builders of many fine fishing schooners. They have similar lines, but the *Ladonna*, as the *Bowditch* was first called, was fitted out in 1923 as a racing yacht for Boston lawyer Homer Loring. She was both fast and seaworthy, following the tradition of the fishing schooners in whose form she was built, and is said to have done well in the 1924 Bermuda Race. She was renamed *Jane Dore* when she was sold to a yachtsman from the New York Yacht Club, and in World War II she was requisitioned by the navy to serve on submarine patrol.

Jane Dore (Bowditch) *in 1937, during her days as a racing yacht, when she carried a staysail rig.*
© *Rosenfeld Collection, Mystic Seaport Museum.*

After the war, the *Jane Dore* was purchased by a fisherman, who took her masts out, installed a wheelhouse, and used her to drag Long Island Sound for groundfish. He worked her through several years, until she was worn out, and then tied her alongside some pilings in Stonington, Connecticut, where she rode up and down with the tide for a couple of years, grounding out in the muck as the water dropped and rising again as it came in.

There, in the early 1960s, her distinctive spoon bow caught the eye of Bob Douglas. She still had the wheelhouse of a powered fishing dragger, but her bow didn't fit; it had an aristocratic look he couldn't ignore. He finally climbed aboard to see what he could see, found the documentation number on her bulkhead, wrote to Washington, and was sent her history. He tracked down the owner and bought the old vessel, rescuing her, like Black Beauty, from her desperate situation. Douglas scrounged around until he found her masts. He replaced those and started some restoration work, and then sold her to Skip Hawkins, who renamed her the *Joseph W. Hawkins*. She was taken to Stonington, Maine, to be fitted for the passenger trade. But these plans didn't work out either, and she was sold again in 1971, this time to a descendant of Nathaniel Bowditch (author of the classic work on navigation) and a partner. After serious rebuilding she was given her present name. She worked for a couple of years, but her owners "got too far ahead of their rebuild," as her present owner, Captain Gib Philbrick, says. Their bankruptcy left an opportunity for Captain Philbrick and his wife, Terry, who bought her in 1975 and have operated her in the windjammer business ever since.

The *Bowditch* was designed to go to weather, and go to weather she does. She likes light airs, and she likes heavy airs (there is a midrange that she's not as happy with, Captain Philbrick confesses). But in a 25-knot breeze he can strike the jib, sheet the jumbo, foresail, and main right in, and she balances herself with the wind flowing smoothly from sail to sail as if she were carrying but a single sail. Then she flies to windward. In a steady breeze, some of the other windjammers can sail along with her, but in the gusty nor'westers of Penobscot Bay, her yachtlike cutaway forefoot gives her a quick handiness to take advantage of the fluky directions of the wind. None of the windjammers is likely to take on a tacking duel, but the *Bowditch* would enjoy it, being sensitive and quick to the helm. Captain Philbrick does admit that some of the coasters fare better off the wind. The *Bowditch's* hull form makes her uncomfortable to sail wing-and-wing; when the straight-keeled vessels track straight, she tends to snap this way and that in the irregularities of the wind and sea. But none is any more graceful than the *Nathaniel Bowditch*, with her elegantly curved sheer and spoon bow. She carried more canvas as a yacht, with a marconi main and staysail rig, but her sail plan today is particularly pretty, her fisherman extending the line of her jib through to the main topmast, where she carries a topsail.

The *Nathaniel Bowditch* had three careers, as yacht, submarine patrol vessel, and fisherman, and then came back to find another, carrying passengers. Captain Philbrick says that you never really own one of these historic vessels, "you pass your time and try to leave them in better shape than you found them." He was reminded of his temporary part in the long life of his vessel one summer recently in Southwest Harbor, when the granddaughter of her 1924 Bermuda Race captain rowed out and asked if she wasn't the old *Ladonna*. In another sixty years will someone row over to her remembering her life under Captain Philbrick?

Nathaniel Bowditch

length: 82'   gross tonnage: 54
beam: 21'6"   sail area: 3,700
draft: 11' (full keel)   rig: main topsail, fisherman
power: 471 Detroit diesel
no. passengers: 24   crew: 4

Roseway

Some four thousand two-masted schooners were constructed in the little town of Essex, Massachusetts, the center of United States two-masted schooner construction. The *Roseway* is one of only six remaining afloat today. She was built in 1925 in the sturdy fashion of a fisherman, complete with a fish hold, but because she was a private yacht special materials and attention were used in her construction. She was taken swordfishing even during her career as a yacht, but after 1941 she went into hard work as a pilot boat and was honored with a medal for serving with distinction during World War II. With a cut-down rig and new GM diesels to replace her huge, old, slow-turning gasoline engines, she worked for over thirty years for the port of Boston, delivering pilots to large ships to guide them into harbor. Boston pilots still remember her for her sea-kindliness and strength.

But the memories are not all romantic. On February 3, 1970, which was her skipper's first day in that role, she was hit by an unforecast storm with winds of over 70 knots and twenty-foot seas.

The Roseway *as a pilot boat. Courtesy of Captain George Sloane, Yankee Schooner Cruises.*

The *Roseway* lost both masts and her generator. Her sails were rags. For several hours the six men aboard struggled amid flailing rigging and washing seas, trying without success to get back to port. They finally anchored, a Coast Guard helicopter took the crew off, and the *Roseway* was left to fend for herself, fully exposed to the weather.

The next day, there she rode quietly, a shambles above decks but dry and sound below. In two weeks, with new masts and new sails, she was back at work.

The last pilot schooner on duty on the East Coast, the *Roseway* was replaced in 1972. She was sold first to a group that hoped to fit her for the passenger business but misjudged the costs, and eventually captains Jim Sharp and Orvil Young purchased her in 1975. She had been stripped below, still had a stubby rig, and her mainsail had been vandalized. They fitted her out for thirty-six passengers, put her to work that summer, and kept improving her over the years. Captain Young carved the eagle she wears today on her bow and built the graceful whitehall she carries as a tender.

The *Roseway* has sailed under captain George Sloane since 1988. She is the only member of the windjammer fleet with international credentials and has represented the state of Maine in several national tall ship festivities. She presently cruises in the Virgin Islands in winter.

The *Roseway* is the longest and heaviest of the two-masted vessels in today's Maine windjammer fleet. Her sawn frames are 8-by-8-inch oak, 16 inches on center, her planking is 3-inch oak, and her ceiling 4-inch longleaf yellow pine. Her sturdy hull is still 99 percent original. Roseway's tanbark sails are a distinctive deep red color, she has the spoon bow of a Gloucester fisherman, and her graceful sheer is emphasized by her dark red waist. Her deep full keel, sleek bow, and feathering propeller make her a strong sailer; she's tough and stiff and loves it when it blows. She doesn't have to shorten sail before 25 knots; then the topsail has to come down only because of the rigging of the lowerable topmast. Her main doesn't get reefed until 30 knots. Given a good breeze on her beam and a reasonable sea, she can cruise along at 12 knots. One time off Grand Manan, carrying the full lowers, Captain Sloane was anxious to get some canvas off, as the wind was gusting to 60 knots, but the *Roseway* took it handily, and the knotmeter reached 15. The *Roseway* still has the big GM diesels the pilots put in her. They turn a single screw through an enormous hydraulic transmission, and they keep her out of trouble.

Captain Sloane says that one of the exciting aspects of skippering the *Roseway* is that he is sailing a historical artifact. He didn't fully realize this until his second summer, when he visited the shipbuilding museum in Essex, Massachusetts, and found patterns from the *Roseway*'s construction. And everywhere they sail, people recognize her. "I knew that was the *Roseway*," said a clockmaker in Charleston, South Carolina. He had welded her watertight bulkheads in Gloucester when she was first being refit for the passenger trade. In the Caribbean, a call came over the radio from an officer on a big cruise ship. He'd known the *Roseway* in Boston, when she was a pilot boat and he was working on tugs in the harbor. In Camden a woman came by the dock and asked to come on board. She looked all around and only then introduced herself as the daughter of the first owner. It was her first time aboard; her father had held the superstition that women brought bad luck to a boat.

Roseway has had a good life, but not because of any superstition; she's earned it. She is a handsome and powerful schooner with a varied history, one whose deep-water credentials are unmistakable.

> ### Roseway
> length: 112'   gross tonnage: 97.4
> beam: 25'   sail area: 5,000
> draft: 12'9" (full keel)   rig: single topsail
> displacement: 190 tons
> power: 2 GM 671 diesels
> no. passengers: 36   crew: 7

Stephen Taber

"This natty little schooner promises to be a good sailer and should bring profits to her owners for years to come," said the *Long Island Gazette* when the *Stephen Taber* was launched in 1871 for the brick trade. She has most certainly done that, hauling freight around Long Island Sound and up the Hudson River for one lifetime, being rebuilt around 1900 and working another full career carrying a variety of goods, landing in Maine in the twenties and continuing her labors. In 1936 Captain Fred Wood, of Orland, bought her and rebuilt her completely. Her graceful sheer restored, she was used for the next several years by Captain Wood and his wife to haul wood on the Penobscot River and in the bay. She often carried so many logs she nearly disappeared underneath them: sixty-three cords at a time, each weighing some two and a half tons.

Captain Boyd Guild, of Castine, bought her in 1946, in the early days of the Maine passenger business, but this was not the *Stephen Taber's* first venture carrying vacationers. The summer of 1900 had been a slow time for carrying cargo on Long Island

The Stephen Taber, *about 1890, at Setauket, New York.*
Mystic Seaport Museum photo.

Sound, so her captain rigged the *Taber's* forward hold with "ladies' facilities," laid out oriental rugs and set up awnings, and took a wealthy family (complete with cook and other servants) for a month's cruise. The log shows that they fell in with a New York Yacht Club cruise to Newport and outsailed a number of the yachts, no doubt providing more pleasure to Captain Halleck and his passengers than to the NYYC members.

Unlike many of the old working schooners, the *Taber* never was converted to power. She has the distinction of being the oldest documented vessel in the United States in continuous service under sail. She is one of the smaller windjammers, sixty-eight feet long and drawing but five feet with centerboard up. She was designed to get up into little coves where there was no wharf and beach out at low tide. Wagons would be run out to her, cargo would be loaded, and she would float off with the tide. She doesn't need to beach out anymore, but her shoal draft gives her access to private coves some of the larger vessels can't reach.

Since she came into the Maine windjammer fleet, the *Stephen Taber* has introduced many a newly certified schooner captain to the emerging passenger cruise world. She served them well, or at least whetted their appetites for more; her name appears in the résumés of many of the skippers of today's windjammers. Yet here she is today, sailing with the fleet, continuing to support herself and provide a living to her owners. Her present masters, captains Ken and Ellen Barnes, don't see her as a stepping stone to anywhere else; for historians like themselves she is a treasure, the quintessential coasting schooner. And she has been recognized as a National Landmark.

The *Taber* has always been known as a lucky boat, lucky for her owners and for herself. Whenever it has been time to do serious maintenance, someone has loved her enough to say "Yes, she's worth it." The Barneses rebuilt her once again in the 1980s, demonstrating that rebuilding the existing schooners in the fleet was economically justified. They used old photographs and a lot of careful eyeballing to recreate the graceful sheerline that the years had taken from her. She is today as strong and capable as she ever was. She likes a good breeze; 15 to 25 knots is her forte. She reefs at 25.

She's presently painted as she was in 1871, a dark green trimmed with black, red, yellow, and white—still natty. Even the angle of her gaffs is jauntily high. She's a saucy little boat with a soul that has enabled her to survive all these years. She is still a family boat, again operated by a husband and wife team much as she was under Captain Wood, whose widow has sailed with the Barneses a number of times. In 1984, wearing a long dress, Mrs. Wood came aboard to celebrate the Bangor sesquicentennial. The Barneses picked her up in Bucksport, where a crowd had gathered to see her off, and the *Taber* sailed up the river. The *Mary Day* and the *J. & E. Riggin* also made the journey. Early the following morning, the three schooners rafted up, flying every flag they could find, yawl boats pushing, and went off with the tide, the last of uncounted gams of schooners to come down the river since the mid-nineteenth century.

The *Taber* still carries the billet head Orvil Young carved for her. As he was carving, an old fellow came along and admired the work, saying, "That's pretty—but she won't sail a damn bit faster."

She doesn't need to.

Stephen Taber

length: 68'   gross tonnage: 53.8

beam: 22'6"   sail area: 3,000

draft: 5' (14'6" board down)

rig: single topmast, no topsails

displacement: 73 tons est.

power: yawl boat

no. passengers: 22   crew: 5

Timberwind

The *Timberwind* was built in Maine for Maine duty, and since her launching as *Portland Pilot* in 1931, she has never been out of Maine waters. Built to carry pilots to and from ships entering or leaving Portland harbor, she was constructed ruggedly to be safe, comfortable, and seaworthy. As launched, she was bald-headed, had no bowsprit, and carried two engines.

Portland Pilot and her crews faced countless vicious winter northeasters when green water as well as spray coming aboard froze to the rigging and had to be chipped off to maintain her stability. She always met the challenge, although in one particularly bitter storm, on February 16, 1958, she suffered her only casualty and was thought lost herself. The wind blew 50 knots, the seas had built to fifteen feet, it was snowing, and *Portland Pilot*'s dory had just left a pilot on the ladder of a fiercely rolling Norwegian ship. Each time the tanker rolled to windward it picked up huge quantities of water,

Portland Pilot (Timberwind) *and her replacement off Portland Head, 1969. Donald E. Johnson photo.*

and as it rolled back, the water fell in tremendous cascades over the leeward side. One such crush of water threw the pilot off the ladder. He was never seen again. The dory also was swamped and sank immediately. The two dorymen were saved by a pair of extraordinary seamen aboard the tanker, who grabbed them and hauled them aboard on the next downward roll of the ship. The weather was getting worse, visibility was zero, and the captain of the schooner, Ted Langzetell, was left alone on *Portland Pilot*. The schooner was blown off in the storm and was not seen or heard from all night. She was feared lost. Somehow, however, she and her captain made it through the storm. The vessel was completely iced over from the seas breaking over her, and Captain Langzetell was soaked and exhausted. He had only been able to stay on deck for short periods for fear of freezing, but *Portland Pilot* came home under her own power nearly a day later.

For thirty-eight years, twenty-four hours a day and in all weather conditions, *Portland Pilot* was on call. When she wasn't hove-to on station fifteen miles offshore, she was in at the dock taking on stores and readying for her next shift. She was finally replaced with a steel powerboat in 1959, but to this day she is fondly remembered by the men who worked on her in Portland. They enjoy coming by Rockport to see her, and although they may chuckle at her fancier paint job and bigger rig, they see that she's still the same working vessel underneath and are pleased to see how well she's cared for.

Captain Bill and Julie Alexander bought *Portland Pilot* soon after she was retired and spent two years rebuilding her for the passenger trade. As they stripped her, they kept finding evidence of the hard life she and her crew had faced, such as elbow-length leather mittens lined with three-eighths-inch wool felt. The Alexanders removed the engines; gave her a taller rig, a topsail, and a yawl boat to help out when the sails couldn't do the job; fitted her out for passengers; and named her *Timberwind*. They preserved as much of her original interior and fittings as they could and found her hull in near perfect condition. Even today, over sixty years after her launching, *Timberwind's* hull is almost entirely original, having been protected by Maine's cold water.

She sailed with the Alexanders for twenty years, and in 1991 she came to Captain Rick Miles and his wife, Beth. Captain Miles likes the feel of the *Timberwind* under sail. She's happiest in 18 to

20 knots breeze. Above that, he strikes the topsail, and she's comfortable to 25 with the four lowers unreefed. The *Timberwind* is particularly handy; Captain Miles enjoys telling how her maneuverability allows him to sneak into an anchorage ahead of the larger vessels that sometimes sail by him in the open water.

The *Timberwind*'s master likes the informal racing that is so common in the fleet. He says the boats like it, too. He knows that a challenger might be a little faster, but there are ten different ways of getting to a destination. Local knowledge of currents, wind conditions, and even rocks and reefs may be more important than speed through the water. And the *Timberwind* can sail a little closer to the wind than some; at times that will make the difference. "No one's going to get by without us having done our best."

Captain Miles has sailed all his life, and to him the *Timberwind* is a dream come true. While he loves all boats, believing in an almost mystical connection between any vessel and her captain, the *Timberwind* is special to him—her history, her physical characteristics, her sailing abilities—and her soul. The *Timberwind* has spent her life with masters who loved her and respected her, and her latest captain is as enamored of her as any.

Timberwind

length: 70'   gross tonnage: 49
beam: 18'6"   sail area: 2,520
draft: 9'7" (full keel)
rig: single topsail
displacement: 85 tons
power: yawl boat
no. passengers: 20   crew: 4

Victory Chimes

The *Victory Chimes* was built as the *Edwin and Maud* in Bethel, Delaware, in 1900 and named for the children of Robert Riggin, her first captain. She is a "ram schooner," thirty-nine of which were built for the waters of Chesapeake Bay. No one agrees on the derivation of the term—it may have been a derogatory phrase referring to the way they passed through the water or through the Delaware River canal—but the ram schooners are said to have earned more money for their owners than any other three-masted schooners. Despite their great size, they were sailed with a crew of just three or four men, since all the sails save one headsail were self-tending. Only the *Victory Chimes* remains, and in fact she is the last original three-masted schooner working in the United States.

The *Edwin and Maud* was designed to carry the maximum load through the Chesapeake and Delaware Canal, being just inches narrower than the canal itself. She is flat-bottomed and flat-sided, and at 170 feet long (including her bowsprit), she is probably just as long as she could be and still get through the locks. She draws only seven and a half feet of water with her centerboard up. She was built sturdy to carry huge cargoes; her skipper, Captain Kip

The Victory Chimes *on the ways, showing her boxy hull shape, designed for maximum cargo capacity.*

Files, says she used to carry sixty or seventy tons on deck alone. She is massively overbuilt for her present job.

The *Edwin and Maud* worked for over forty years carrying cargo and for several years carrying passengers on the Chesapeake before Captain Boyd Guild brought her to Maine in 1954 and gave her the name *Victory Chimes*. She cruised in Maine for thirty years.

In 1985 she was purchased and taken to the Great Lakes, where she came on hard times and was ultimately repossessed by a Duluth bank. Her next stop was home on the Chesapeake, where she was offered for sale. There she sat, her pumps running around the clock to keep her afloat, and was finally rescued when Thomas Monaghan of Domino's Pizza bought her. During the three years Domino's owned her, a great deal of careful restoration work was done.

The *Victory Chimes*'s three masts stand some eighty feet over the water. Replacing one of these is not an easy matter, at least not in the original single-log style. A straight tree 110 feet tall is required to get the necessary length a full twenty-one inches in diameter. (Federal protection of the endangered spotted owl made the purchase of such a spar next to impossible, according to Captain Files.) But there was no skimping on materials during her restoration. She is now about 70 percent new, and the work was done right.

Much to the distress of folks who knew her as the *Victory Chimes*, the vessel carried the name *Domino Effect* during the years she belonged to Domino's. (On the Chesapeake people are just as upset by the name *Victory Chimes*, since for fifty-four years she had been well known there as the *Edwin and Maud*. Edwin Riggin, for whom she was named, lived in Maryland and was running a grocery store as recently as 1960.) But while many people in Maine remember Domino's Pizza only for having changed the vessel's name, Domino's should be remembered for having saved the *Victory Chimes*'s life.

In 1990, still carrying the Domino's Pizza flag, she came back to Rockland and the windjammer business, skippered by Captain Files. A year later, Captain Files and Captain Paul de Gaeta purchased her and rechristened her the *Victory Chimes*.

To this day she has no inboard auxiliary power, depending on her yawl boat to move her in close quarters or at times with no wind. As was common in sailing vessels of her day, she does have a 1916 donkey engine forward to power the anchor windlass. Each of her cabins has hot and cold running water, and she has hot-air heat below.

The *Victory Chimes* is no greyhound, but Captain Files says she is a relatively easy boat to sail. Sometimes she seems even longer than she is, though, particularly in tight conditions, and she doesn't stop easily once she's started. She makes a lot of leeway going to weather. But in general, she is surprisingly handy. In light airs she'll come about more easily than would a two-master of her size because the leverage of her mizzen pushes her right through the wind. She likes a good breeze—18 or 20 knots is ideal—and her size and heft make her an impressive lady under way. And Captain Files reports that once in a while she can get past even the fastest members of the fleet, if the breeze is strong enough that they've had to bring in their topsails and the slant of wind is just right. "She can make over ten knots—though there's no water left in the bay when we've gone through."

Victory Chimes

length: 132'   gross tonnage: 208

beam: 25'   sail area: 6,500

draft: 7'6" (18' board down)

rig: three-masted, bald-headed

displacement: 395 tons est.

power: yawl boat

no. passengers: 44   crew: 9

Wendameen

    The first of many schooner yachts from the drawing board of John Alden, the *Wendameen* was built in East Boothbay, Maine, in 1912. Thought to be one of the earliest yachts to carry auxiliary power, she is heavier and beamier than many of her contemporaries, yet still maintains a refined and elegant appearance.

The *Wendameen* was designed for Chester Bliss, owner of the Boston and Albany Railroad and the Chapin National Bank. He sailed her on Long Island Sound with his family and friends. In 1916, the *Wendameen* was sold to the Uihlein family of Milwaukee, owners of the Schlitz breweries. With the coming of Prohibition, the Wendameen was moved to Chicago, where her new owner was a colorful lawyer named L'Amoreaux, who cruised with his family

The Wendameen *in the 1920s. Courtesy of Captain Neal Parker.*

for ten years. Each year L'Amoreaux entered the *Wendameen* in the Mackinac race, which took him close to Canada and gave him the opportunity to refill his liquor cabinets. L'Amoreaux brought the *Wendameen* back to Long Island sound, intending to trade her for a powerboat that better suited his failing health, but he died before the transaction took place. The *Wendameen* became the property of yacht broker G.W. Ford, of City Island, New York, who carefully labeled and stored all her gear when he hauled her for the winter at a local yard. The Depression interfered with the resale of the boat. Then came World War II. Ford chose to leave the *Wendameen* laid up rather than allow her to be requisitioned for submarine patrol. He had dreams of retiring onto her, and did two major overhauls of the schooner (in 1936 and 1963) at a cost of a quarter of a million dollars. In 1984, when Ford was 92 years old, the shipyard closed where *Wendameen* was stored. Ford had neither retired nor ever sailed his schooner, but he abandoned his own hopes and launched her, offering her for sale. The *Wendameen* came adrift in a spring storm, suffering serious damage; a purchaser attempted repairs, but gave up and left her stuck in a mud bank in western Connecticut.

The *Wendameen's* present owner, Captain Neal Parker, found her in the mud in 1986, as if she were just waiting to make her comeback. He was determined to restore her to her original glory. Although it took years, he accomplished just that. Captain Parker found her gear right where it had been stored by Mr. Ford in 1933. He used a great number of fittings and was even able to utilize one original staysail during his first two seasons. Another thread connects her past to her present: a caulker worked on her in 1936 in City Island; in 1976, still in City Island, his son caulked her; and in 1989 the son, who had since moved to Maine, again worked on her.

Although a great deal of the boat had to be replaced, she still exudes much of her early history. The *Wendameen* looks distinguished with her blue hull and varnished cockpit, skylights, and trim. Below, as when first launched, the appointments are airy, with white painted panels and mahogany trim. Simple green velvet cushions in the saloon evoke the charm of an older time.

Captain Parker has collected scrap books of pictures and

stories about the *Wendameen* and her former owners. He enjoys sharing these as if they were his own memories and not just those of his boat. "Late at night you feel their shadows around you." An old Victor gramophone is a part of the equipment aboard; the George Gershwin recording of "Rhapsody in Blue" brings applause every time. Captain Parker says the *Wendameen* is a time machine taking her guests into the early part of this century for a yachting adventure. Or perhaps back in their own lives; couples who haven't thought to hold hands in ten years somehow end up sitting close together alone on deck at night, and social engagements from fifty years back are brought to the minds of the more elderly guests.

Sailing is fun on the *Wendameen*. She makes good time in any kind of weather, finding it easy to reach 7 knots, and clocking 12 on occasion. She likes light air or heavy, though 15 to 20 knots is her choice.

Of all the older members of the fleet, only the *Wendameen* has never been converted from anything else. As Captain Parker says, today she does "the job she was originally designed for: sailing like a son of a gun and taking people out to have a good time."

Wendameen

length: 67'   gross tonnage: 47
beam: 17'6"   sail area: 2,400
draft: 9' (full keel)
rig: bald-headed; round, tapered, extended mastheads
displacement: 52 tons
power: 80-hp diesel
no. passengers: 14   crew: 4

Identifying the Windjammers

Identifying a vessel can be difficult from a distance, but the more familiar one becomes, the easier it is. The sail plan is the clearest identifier; it is the first thing visible, and also each vessel's sail plan is just a little different from every other's. Not only is there variety in terms of the particular sails carried—topsails or fishermen, for instance—but the overall impression can be distinctive. Some schooners have very solid-looking rigs while others show a lot of daylight.

The following descriptions, and the chart on pages 96–97, explain how to distinguish the individual members of the windjammer fleet even from a distance. (See the Glossary, page 124, for help with terminology.)

Angelique

The first step is to determine whether a vessel is a schooner, a ketch, a brigantine, or something else. All but one in the windjammer fleet are schooners (if it's a dark-sailed ketch, it's probably *Angelique*). The next step is to determine whether her sails are gaff-rigged, or whether she carries one or more marconi sails, a square sail, or a staysail.

Assuming that it's gaff-rigged (as all the windjammer fleet members are), the third step is to look for topsails or topmasts. The bald-headed schooners—with no topsails—are the *Bowdoin* (the

Bowdoin

American Eagle

Mercantile

Grace Bailey

Wendameen

J. & E. Riggin

Victory Chimes

only knockabout rig in the lot), *American Eagle* (with a very long main boom and correspondingly large mainsail, and extreme sheer), *Mercantile* (green hull with tan sails), *Grace Bailey* (also green, but with white sails), *Wendameen* (blue hull, mainmast and sail significantly taller than her fore), and of course *Victory Chimes* (with her three masts, she's most easily identified).

Isaac H. Evans

Timberwind

Nathaniel Bowditch

Roseway

Carrying a single topmast and topsail are the *Timberwind* (main more angled, leech of topsail nearly a continuation of main's, smaller headsails, spoon bow), *Isaac H. Evans* (more nearly rectangular main, topsail makes clearly broken line, larger headsails, clipper bow), *Nathaniel Bowditch* (black hull, also carries a fisherman), and *Roseway*

Stephen Taber

(red sails). The *Stephen Taber* has a single topmast flying a huge pennant, no topsail, and a very airy rig, and her boom overhangs her stern proportionately more than the others'.

Lewis R. French

Heritage

Mary Day

The *Lewis R. French* and the *Heritage* have two topmasts and main and jib topsails (but no fore topsail). With all sails flying, they look a little as if a tooth were missing. The *French* has a gray hull; *Heritage* is longer and has distinctive striping.

Only *Mary Day* carries main, fore, and jib topsails.

Identification Chart for the Vessels in the

Vessel Name; Hails From	Length; Beam; Draft	Tops	Rig (if unusual); No. of Headsails
American Eagle Rockland	92'L; 20'b; 11'4"d	bald	2 headsails
Angelique Camden	95'L; 23'7"b; 11'6"d	main & mizzen topsails	ketch; 4 headsails
Bowdoin Castine	88'L; 22'b; 9'6"d	bald	knockabout; 2 headsails
Grace Bailey Camden	80'L; 23'6"b; 7'd	bald	2 headsails
Heritage Rockland	94'L; 24'b; 8'd	2 topmasts, main topsail	3 headsails
Isaac H. Evans Rockland	65'L; 20'b; 6'd	1 topmast, main topsail	2 headsails
J. & E. Riggin Rockland	89'L; 22'6"b; 7'd	bald	2 headsails
Lewis R. French Rockland	64'L; 19'b; 7'6"d	2 topmasts, main topsail	3 headsails
Mary Day Camden	90'L; 23'6"b; 7'd	main and fore topsails	3 headsails
Mercantile Camden	80'L; 22'b; 6'7"d	bald	2 headsails
Nathaniel Bowditch Cape Rosier	82'L; 21'6"b; 11'd	1 topmast, main topsail, fisherman	2 headsails
Roseway Camden	112'L; 25'b; 12'9"d	1 topmast, main topsail	2 headsails
Stephen Taber Rockland	68'L; 22'6"b; 5'd	1 topmast, no topsail	2 headsails
Timberwind Rockport	70'L; 18'6"b; 9'7"d	1 topmast, main topsail	2 headsails
Victory Chimes Rockland	132'L; 25'b; 7'6"d	bald	3-masted; 3 headsails
Wendameen Rockland	67'L; 17'6"b; 9'd	bald; mainmast much taller than foremast	pole-masted; 2 headsails

Maine Windjammer Fleet, Including Bowdoin

Bow Appearance	Paint (as of 1992)	Distinguishing Characteristics	Power Source
steep spoon; bowsprit	lt. gray, dk. blue waist	huge main; extreme sheer; masthead trim balls; near-round transom	engine
plumb; sprit, jib boom	green, white waist	ketch; dk. brown sails; steel hull; fantail stern	engine
spoon; no bowsprit	all white	barrel on foremast	engine
clipper; bowsprit	green, white waist, natural cabin tops, white sails	shallow gaff angle; long, low quarter rail; 2 windows in main cabin	yawl boat
clipper; sprit, jib boom	ivory, white waist, blue, red, and black stripes	2 topmasts; 1 topsail; black and gold trailboard	yawl boat
clipper; sprit, jib boom	white, red stripe	low, straight sheer; very long quarter rail	yawl boat
spoon; bowsprit	black, red stripe, white rail & houses	bald, capped mastheads; black bowsprit; low freeboard	engine
clipper; bowsprit	gray, black waist, red log rail	only dk. gray schooner in fleet; 2 topmasts, 1 topsail	yawl boat
clipper; bowsprit	very lt. gray, white waist	2 topsails; high sides and bulwarks nearly same color	yawl boat
clipper; bowsprit	green, white waist, lt. green cabin tops	shallow gaff angle; short, high quarter rail; 3 windows in main cabin	yawl boat
spoon; bowsprit	black	black boats on davits, both sides; fisherman sail	engine
spoon; bowsprit; gold eagle	cream, dk. red waist	1 topsail; dk. red sails; hull long for mast height	engine
clipper; bowsprit	dk. green, yellow stripe, black waist	pennant only on topmast; very dark; clipper bow; long boom overhang	yawl boat
steep spoon; bowsprit	white, blue waist	appears low-sided; nearly plumb bow	yawl boat
clipper; bowsprit	green, white waist	3 masts	yawl boat
spoon; bowsprit	blue	only blue hull in fleet; refined spars; fine, yachty transom	engine

Other Schooners and Historic Vessels Seen in Maine Waters

Many other interesting and historic vessels visit Maine waters regularly or from time to time. Among them are the following, all of which are two-masted, gaff-rigged wooden schooners with bowsprit except as otherwise noted.

Adventure, Gloucester, Massachusetts

Courtesy of Gloucester Adventure, Inc.

Knockabout schooner, 121'6" by 24'6" by 13'9". 130 tons gross, displacement 257 tons, sail area 6,500 square feet, including main topsail. Built as an auxiliary schooner on the lines of the *Oretha F*.

Spinney, a McManus design, in 1926 in Essex, Massachusetts. *Adventure* fished the Grand Banks from Gloucester carrying twenty-seven men and a dozen dories. Under her second owner, Captain Leo Hynes, she broke all records for haddock, bringing home $3.5 million worth of fish in the nineteen years of his ownership. In 1953 she was the last remaining dory-fishing schooner out of Gloucester, and Captain Hynes retired her only for lack of crew. The following year, minus her engine, she joined the Maine windjammer fleet for a thirty-three year hitch carrying thirty-seven passengers, eight crew, and a yawl boat. In 1988 she was donated by Captain Jim Sharp, her owner for most of her windjammer days, to the people of Gloucester; she is now maintained by the nonprofit Gloucester Adventure, Inc., whose mission includes heightening public awareness of the importance of Gloucester in the American fishing industry. They have given *Adventure* her original black paint and plan to rebuild her for recertification for carrying passengers. Overnight accommodations aboard are available at pierside.

Annie McGee, Rockland, Maine

Pinky, 28' by 9' by 6', sail area 800 square feet. 11-horsepower diesel. The *Annie McGee* was built in the 1950s by an employee at

Bath Iron Works in his spare time. Many of her original fittings were left over from BIW projects, including her ballast, 3500 pounds of cast iron, smuggled out bit by bit in a lunch pail. Launched in 1957, *Annie McGee* never made the trip to Europe that her builder had intended, though he sailed her for nearly twenty years before he died. In 1986 her present owner, Captain "Yo" Yosarian, bought her. He has rebuilt about 50 percent of the vessel, correcting various problems caused by the odd mix of materials in her original construction. She is one of the few vessels on the Maine coast to sport an oculus, an eye painted on her bow, which is a traditional sign of good luck in the Far East. The *Annie McGee* carries six passengers and is available for day charters.

Appledore, Portsmouth, New Hampshire

Staysail schooner, 49' by 12'6" by 6'6", 16 tons gross, sail area 1400 square feet in marconi main, gaff foresail, two headsails, and fisherman. 25-horsepower Penta diesel engine. The first of Herb Smith's five *Appledores*, she was designed by D.C. "Bud" McIntosh and built of native New Hampshire woods by him and Smith. She was launched in 1972 and taken to the West Indies for the making of the video *Romantic Caribbean Islands*. Captain Smith sold her in 1977; presently she is available for a variety of trips. Owned by Captain Rick Bates.

Appledore [II], Camden, Maine

65' by 19' by 9'6", displacement 67 tons. Sail area 2,070 square feet in the four lowers. Cummins diesel engine. Captain Herb Smith's second schooner designed by Bud McIntosh, her hull was built in 1978 at the Gamage yard in South Bristol, Maine. She was fitted out by Captain Smith, who made a global circumnavigation with her before she was put into day and charter work. Accommodates twenty-six overnight, forty-nine on day sails, which she now offers out of Camden in summer and Key West in winter. John McKean, captain.

(The third and fourth *Appledores* are currently berthed in Rockport, Massachusetts, and on the Great Lakes, respectively.)

Appledore V, Boothbay Harbor, Maine

58' by 14' by 7', displacement 34 tons, sail area 1700 square feet, including main topsail. 90-horsepower Ford diesel engine. Steel schooner of traditional lines designed by Bud McIntosh and launched in 1992 by Captain Herb Smith. Operated by the Smith family for charter and day trips.

Bay Lady, Bar Harbor, Maine

65' by 18' by 6'6". Steel schooner built in 1988 in East Boothbay, Maine, specifically for short-trip passenger business. Owned by Frenchman Bay Company.

Bill of Rights, Philadelphia, Pennsylvania

94'10" by 23'10" by 9'6", sail area 4,445 square feet, including two topsails. Diesel auxiliary. Built with exceptional care and fine detail in 1971 as an unpowered private yacht at the Harvey Gamage yard in South Bristol, Maine. Acquired in 1987 by VisionQuest, which provides programs for adjudicated delinquent youth.

Bluenose II, Halifax, Nova Scotia

143' by 27' by 16', 285 tons displacement, sail area 12,550 square feet in main, foresail, three headsails, two topsails, and fisherman. 2 Caterpillar diesels. Built in 1963 in Lunenburg, Nova Scotia, as a private yacht for Olands Ltd. beer brewers, she is a reproduction in hull and rig of the original Canadian *Bluenose*, generally accepted to have been the fastest of the racing fishermen. These racing vessels were better sailers but poorer freighters than the typical fuller-formed fishing schooners. *Bluenose II* has been clocked at 18 knots under sail, and her engines allow her to cruise

Courtesy of Nova Scotia Dept. of Tourism and Culture.

at 12 knots. She is constructed of native softwoods, with the exception of her keel and stem. These are of good oak left over from the construction at the same yard of the reproduction *Bounty* for the movie *Mutiny on the Bounty*, and have made possible a longer life than might otherwise have been the case, since the native softwoods are not long lasting. Plans have been made to replace this vessel, again in identical form to the original Bluenose in hull and rig, but using United States white oak. *Bluenose II* was donated to the province of Nova Scotia in 1971 and is used to promote the province for business and tourism.

Brilliant, Mystic, Connecticut

61'6" by 14'8" by 8'10", sail area 2,417 square feet. White auxiliary schooner yacht designed by Sparkman & Stephens, built in 1932. Although designed for deep-water cruising, she was a competitive racer as well. In 1933 she made a transatlantic passage in record time for a vessel her size, averaging over 9 knots the whole way. Originally gaff-rigged on main and fore, she was re-

rigged with her present marconi main after World War II, during which she served on submarine patrol. She is now operated by Mystic Seaport as a sail training vessel.

Corwith Cramer, Woods Hole, Massachusetts

Brigantine, 98' by 26' by 13', 158 tons gross, displacement 260 tons, sail area 7,800 square feet. 500-horsepower diesel auxiliary. Complement thirty-six, including ten professional staff (captain, other officers, engineer, steward, and scientists). She was built in 1987 in Spain for Sea Education Association, the present owners, and logged an average of ten thousand nautical miles in each of the next five years. She carries enough stores for six weeks at sea. Including fuel, water, and food, and the people themselves, she puts on some sixty tons before departure. Sea Education Association offers college-level semester-long oceanography and maritime programs as well as shorter educational seminars for a variety of participants.

Ernestina, New Bedford, Massachusetts

Courtesy of the Ernestina-Morrissey Historical Assn.

106' by 24'5" by 13', displacement 240 tons, sail area 8,323 square feet, including main and fore topsails and fisherman. Formerly the *Effie M. Morrissey*, she was designed by George M. McClain and built in Essex, Massachusetts, in 1894 and is the oldest surviving Grand Banks fishing schooner. Although said to have been built along the lines of the *Fredonia*, in fact she's more of a workhorse. She fished the Grand Banks for eighteen years, bringing in up to two hundred thousand pounds of fish each trip. She was later converted to carry cargo on the Labrador run. In

1924 she was purchased by Robert A. Bartlett, who made twenty exploratory voyages to the Arctic with her; in 1940 she reached 80°22' north latitude. After service off Greenland in World War II and a brief and disastrous career as a private yacht, she was taken in 1948 to the Cape Verde Islands, where she was renamed *Ernestina* and used as a general carrier into the mid-sixties. Among other payloads were the last immigrants—and perhaps the only voluntary black immigrants—to arrive in the United States in a commercial sailing vessel. After suffering serious damage in 1976, she was rebuilt by the Cape Verdians with the help of some of the Americans who as young men had sailed aboard her in the Arctic, and was donated to the United States by the new West African Republic of Cape Verde in 1982. The Commonwealth of Massachusetts operates her as a sail training vessel.

Flying Fish, Islesboro, Maine

45' by 12'6" by 7'1", sail area 1500 square feet. Black hull, raked masts, dark red sails, gold fish at the bow and stern. Built as a yacht in 1936, she appeared in the movie *Carousel*. She is used for chartering and educational projects. Captain Earl MacKenzie, owner.

Francis Todd, Cherryfield, Maine

78' by 17'6" by 7'6", 55 tons gross, estimated displacement 85 tons, estimated sail area 3,000 square feet. 671 diesel. Former carrier/seiner *Lou Ann*, built in 1947 in Thomaston, Maine. At this writing, she is being converted to schooner rig for day and overnight passenger service. Captain Steve Pagels, owner.

Gazela of Philadelphia, Philadelphia, Pennsylvania

Courtesy of the Philadelphia Ship Preservation Guild.

Barkentine, 177' overall by 27' by 17', displacement 636 tons, sail area 11,000 square feet. 385-horsepower auxiliary engine. Last of the wooden Portuguese sailing fishermen, and the largest original wooden square-rigger still sailing. Built in 1883, *Gazela* sailed from Portugal to the Grand Banks for six months every year from 1900 until 1969, carrying forty men and thirty-five dories and bringing back 350 tons of salt cod each trip. In 1971 she was purchased to become Philadelphia's tall ship. She had significant rebuilding in 1992, but has always been copper clad below the waterline, and her planking is still in excellent condition. She was constructed of "stone pine" and "maritime pine" said to have been planted by Portugal's Prince Henry the Navigator in the fifteenth century. Today she sails with a crew of twenty-four to thirty-six—all volunteer, including the captain. Owned and operated by the nonprofit Philadelphia Ship Preservation Guild.

Harvey Gamage, Boston, Massachusetts

95' by 24' by 10', sail area 4,200 square feet. 120-horsepower diesel engine. Built for the passenger trade in 1973 in South Bristol, Maine, using the same lofting as the *Bill of Rights*. Owned and

operated by Eben Whitcomb of Dirigo Cruises, Clinton, Connecticut, for pleasure and educational cruises from Boston, Bar
Harbor, and St. Thomas. Carries thirty-two passengers, seven crew.

Maine, Bath, Maine

Pinky, 39' by 13' by 6', sail area approximately 1,000 square
feet. Owned by and built at the Maine Maritime Museum from a
half model of a pinky built in East Boothbay in the 1830s and
typical of the type as to rig, deck, and details. Launched in 1985.
On display and occasionally sailed by apprentices at the Apprenticeshop in Bath in festivities up and down the Maine coast.

Mistress, Camden, Maine

46' by 13'6" by 6'. Diesel auxiliary. Her construction was begun
on Deer Isle as a backyard project in 1960 by a man who planned
to use her privately. She was purchased in 1966 and fitted out for
crewed charter for three couples in separate cabins, each with its
own head. Over the years *Mistress* has been owned by the various
owners of *Mercantile* and *Mattie/Grace Bailey*, presently Captain

Ray Williamson. She was stretched six feet in the stern in 1992 as part of a full rebuild.

Natalie Todd, Cherryfield, Maine

Three-masted schooner, 101' by 21' by 10', sail area 3,900 square feet; displacement 173 tons. 671 diesel engine. She was built in 1941 in Brooklyn, New York, as the two-masted auxiliary schooner-dragger *Virginia*, transitional between sail and full power. She was used under a variety of names carrying cargo and as an eastern-rig dragger until 1986, when she was bought by Captain Steve Pagels, her present owner, who rebuilt and renamed her and offers day sails out of Bar Harbor.

New Way, Philadelphia, Pennsylvania

Courtesy of VisionQuest. Bob Sobolovitch photo.

92' by 23' by 7'9", 92 tons gross, displacement 115 tons, sail area 5,290 square feet, including main topsail. Twin diesels. Built in 1939 as the *Western Union* to lay and repair underwater telephone and telegraph cable off Florida. Acquired in 1984 by VisionQuest (see entry for *Bill of Rights*).

Niagara, Erie, Pennsylvania

Courtesy of the Pennsylvania Historical & Museum Commission.

Brig, 116' by 32' by 10', displacement 295 tons, sail area 12,665 square feet. Twin diesels. Originally built in Erie during the war of 1812, the *Niagara* was Commander Oliver Hazard Perry's relief flagship in the Battle of Lake Erie in 1813. Aboard her, he broke the British battle line, forcing the surrender of the British naval forces. It was from the deck of the *Niagara* that Perry sent the famous message, "We have met the enemy, and they are ours." She served but seven years longer and then was scuttled. In commemoration of the battle she was raised and fully rebuilt in the early 1900s. After reconstruction in 1988, a few original timbers and parts still remain. She serves today as the flagship of the state of Pennsylvania. Although the original vessel carried 155 men in 1813, today she sails with a professional crew of twelve to sixteen, and twenty volunteers.

Ocean Star, Portland, Maine

74' by 19' by 9', gross 65 tons, displacement 60 tons. Sail area approximately 3,000 square feet in marconi main, gaff fore, 3 headsails, and fisherman on pole masts. 200-horsepower Caterpillar diesel engine and an auxiliary diesel engine for electrical needs. Designed to look traditional, she has been built of quarter-inch

steel plate with five independent watertight compartments.
Launched in 1991, she is dedicated to teaching navigation of all
types, and sails the Atlantic coast and islands carrying six students
and six crew. Although she is relatively spartan below, she is well
set up for her mission, the most noticeable feature perhaps being
her eight-foot-long chart table. She is affiliated with and operated
on behalf of *Ocean Navigator* magazine.

Olad, Camden, Maine

47' by 12'6" by 6'6", sail area 1,500 square feet. Diesel auxiliary.
Designed for his own use by Horace Crosby and built in 1929 at the
Crosby yard in Osterville, Massachusetts. Subsequently *Olad* was in
the charter trade in the Caribbean, Bermuda, and Provincetown,
Massachusetts. Since 1987, Captain John Nugent has offered day
sails from Camden.

Perseverance, Rockport, Maine

Pinky, 26' by 8'6" by 4'. Diesel auxiliary. Built at the
Apprenticeshop in Rockport and launched in 1984. She is built on
lines taken by Howard Chapell and Lincoln Colcord from a
Penobscot fishing pinky they referred to as the Prospect Marsh

Pinky. Her rig and deck layout were designed by Bob Baker, who dated the original vessel to the 1840s. She was the first boat laid down and lofted at the Apprenticeshop, although for financial reasons it was two years before she could be completed. Owned by Tod and Lance Lee, *Perseverance* is operated as a sail training vessel for the Atlantic Challenge Foundation.

Pride of Baltimore II, Baltimore, Maryland

Topsail schooner designed after the Baltimore clippers of the early nineteenth century, 99'8" by 26'5" by 12'4", displacement

185.5 tons, sail area 10,000 square feet. Twin Caterpillar diesels. Built to replace the original *Pride of Baltimore*, lost at sea in 1986, she conforms to Coast Guard regulations for carrying passengers. With a professional paid crew of twelve, the *Pride* is seen on both sides of the Atlantic as a goodwill ambassador for the city of Baltimore and the state of Maryland, promoting economic development and tourism. She is painted in the black and yellow of the state flower, the black-eyed susan, and the extreme rake of her masts is distinctive.

Rachel B. Jackson, Southwest Harbor, Maine

Topsail schooner, 55' by 16' by 8', gross tonnage 52, sail area 2,500 square feet, including main and jib topsails, squaresail, and fisherman. 115-horsepower Westerbeke diesel. Constructed in the traditional manner from plans drafted in 1890. Her hull was built in Jonesport, then she was finished in Freeport and launched in 1982. She was operated as a sail training vessel by Mystic Seaport in Mystic, Connecticut, and then sold to an individual who made a three-year circumnavigation in her. Purchased in 1992 by Captain Jeff Crafts, who offers various trips from Southwest Harbor.

Sherman Zwicker, Boothbay Harbor, Maine

142' by 26' by 13'6". Huge 320-horsepower Fairbanks Morse engine. One of the last Grand Banks schooners built (in the same yard as the *Bluenose*), the *Zwicker* is typical of the Canadian fish freighters, being fuller forward and in the forefoot than the *Bluenose*. She was launched in Lunenburg, Nova Scotia, in 1942. Although she carried steadying sails for her short knockabout rig, her main source of power was her engine, which to this day drives the propeller directly, with no gear box. (To go backward, the crew must shut down the engine, reverse the cam, and restart.) The *Zwicker* fished until the late 1960s, carrying twenty-four fishermen, twelve dories, and a crew of four (captain, engineer, cook, and boy.) Her hold had a capacity of 320,000 pounds of fish, and she carried more stacked on deck. She made three trips to the Grand Banks each year, and in fall and winter carried salt fish to South America, bringing salt back. The *Sherman Zwicker* is now maintained for display by the Grand Banks Schooner Museum of Boothbay, and when she isn't at the various festivities she attends on the East Coast and in the Maritimes, she is often berthed at Maine Maritime Museum, Bath.

Spirit of Massachusetts, Boston, Massachusetts

100' by 24' by 10'5", 90 tons gross, sail area 7,000 square feet, including main and jib topsails and fisherman. 235-horsepower diesel. Launched at Charlestown Navy Yard in 1984, she is modeled on the lines of the *Fredonia*, the famous Gloucester fisherman schooner of 1889. Serves as sail training vessel, taking charters as well. In winter she sails in the Caribbean. Twenty overnight passengers, ten crew. Owned by New England Historic Seaport.

Summertime, Brooklin, Maine

Pinky, 52'9" by 13'7" by 7', net tonnage 29, displacement 37 tons, sail area 1700 square feet in three lower sails; sometimes flies a fisherman. Auxiliary diesel engine. She was built in the traditional manner from lines Howard Chapelle took off a model in Portland dating to the 1830s. *Summertime* is ruggedly constructed of the same types of wood as early nineteenth-century pinkies: native oak, tamarack, and locust. She is the largest pinky sailing today and probably one of the larger ones ever built. Captains Bill Brown and George Allen and a number of young volunteers constructed her over the course of several winters, launching her in 1986. Licensed for seven passengers overnight, twenty day sailing. Captain Brown offers a variety of trips from Rockland.

Surprise, Camden, Maine

44' by 12' by 6'7", designed by Thomas McManus, innovative designer of fishing schooners, and built in Rockport, Massachusetts, in 1918 as a private yacht for Martin Catinhorn, who sailed and raced her from Long Island Sound for forty-five years. She has never been known by another name. Current owners Captain Jack and Barbara Moore and their Siamese cat have been offering day sails from Camden since 1986.

Sylvina W. Beal, Mystic, Connecticut

Courtesy of Captain Geoffrey Jones.

Knockabout schooner, 80' by 17'3" by 8', 46 gross tons, displacement 60 tons, sail area 2,500 square feet in a bald-headed rig. 80-horsepower Perkins diesel. Oak on oak, treenail fastened, she was built in East Boothbay, Maine, in 1911 as an auxiliary schooner sardine carrier. In the mid-1930s her sail area was cut back and she was given a larger engine and a wheelhouse. For over sixty years she worked in various aspects of the fishing business, carrying fish and other products out of ports from Nova Scotia to Massachusetts. In the late 1970s she was entirely rebuilt to carry sardines to a Canadian packing plant planned for Rockland. When the plant didn't open, the *Beal* was seized for unpaid debt. Captain John Worth bought her in 1980, restored her sailing rig, replaced her huge diesel engines with a small auxiliary, and installed passenger accommodations. She carried passengers for five years from Belfast and another four from Portland before her present owner, Captain Geoffrey Jones, brought her to Mystic. She is fitted out in traditional style with canvas sails, manila lines, and a coal stove, and carries eighteen overnight passengers and four crew.

Tabor Boy, Marion, Massachusetts

Steel schooner, 92' by 21'9" by 10'6", sail area 6,800 square feet in marconi main, gaff foresail, fore staysail, and inner and outer jibs. 330-horsepower diesel engine. Built in Amsterdam in 1914, she worked as a Dutch North Sea pilot schooner until 1923. Under the name of *Bestevaer*, she sailed as a Dutch Merchant Service school ship and in World War II was captured by the Germans during their occupation of the Netherlands. Returned to Holland after the war, she was purchased by American Ralph C. Allen, who presented her to Tabor Academy in 1954. The academy has sailed her since then in a variety of programs in Marion, the Caribbean, and Maine. Berths twenty-two, including six crew.

Westward, Woods Hole, Massachusetts

Staysail schooner, 95' by 21'6"by 12'6", 139 tons, sail area 7,000 square feet, including single squaresail. 500-horsepower diesel auxiliary. Complement: thirty-five, including ten professional staff. Designed along the lines of a North Sea pilot schooner by Eldredge-McInnis and built as a yacht in 1961. Owned and

1972 by Sea Education Association (see entry for the *Corwith Cramer*).

When and If, Vineyard Haven, Massachusetts

Courtesy of Boutilier Photos.

63'5" by 15' by 9', sail area 1,771 square feet. Diesel auxiliary. Designed by John Alden, built for General George S. Patton in

Wiscasset, Maine, in 1939. Carrying a squaresail as originally rigged, she now has a standard marconi schooner rig. She was so seriously damaged in a storm in 1990 that she was feared beyond repair, but her original construction was sufficiently strong that rebuilding was possible and justified. Formerly owned by the Landmark School in Beverly, Massachusetts, she now belongs to James Mairs, of New York, and Gannon and Benjamin, wooden-boat builders of Vineyard Haven. The Landmark School will continue to sail her, and she is available for charter.

DEFINITIONS OF NAUTICAL TERMS

aft: toward the rear of the boat, astern

athwartships: across the vessel

bald-headed: having no topsails

barkentine: vessel of three or more masts, the foremost of which carries square sails and the others fore-and-aft rigged

beam: the breadth of the vessel

bilge: lowest part of the vessel's interior

billet head: wooden scroll used in place of a figurehead

block: a pulley used in a vessel's rig

bow: the forward part of a vessel

brigantine: two-masted vessel, the foremast carrying square sails, the main fore-and-aft rigged

bulkhead: vertical partition that strengthens or divides the hull

bulwark: the inside of a vessel's hull above the deck

ceiling: planking on the inside of the frame

centerboard: a board that can be lowered to provide resistance to the sideways movement of a vessel, as does a keel, but with the advantage that it can be raised to allow the vessel to navigate shallow water

club: a spar on the foot of a jib or headsail

coach house: small structure on deck over the companionway

coaster: vessel that carried cargo from one coastal port to another; not a deep-water vessel

companionway: ladder or stairway from deck to living quarters

crosstrees: horizontal struts on the mast to spread the shrouds (rigging)

davits: arms extending over the side or stern to carry a small boat

displacement: the actual weight of a vessel (measured in long tons by the weight of water she displaces when floating)

donkey engine: an engine on deck that provides power for raising the anchor or sails or cargo; does not provide power to propel the vessel

draft: the vertical distance from the surface of the water to the deepest part of the vessel's keel

eastern-rig dragger: a fishing vessel that sets dragging gear off the side of the vessel (as opposed to Western, stern-rigged)

fathom: six feet

feathering props: propellers with blades that rotate on their individual axes, when not in use, in order to decrease water resistance

fly rail: open rail around the quarterdeck

fo'c'sle: the cabin farthest forward, often the crew's quarters

fore: toward the bow of the vessel

fore-and-aft sails: sails set from a vertical mast or stay, the normal position being parallel to the keel, as opposed to square-rigged

forefoot: the forward section of a full keel

freeboard: the portion of the hull above water.

gaff rig: quadrilateral lower sails, luff attached to the mast, with a spar above (gaff) and usually a boom below

galley: kitchen

gam: vessels tied together for a visit or friendly get-together

going to weather: see "on the wind"

halyard: a line used to hoist sails, flags, or spars

head: toilet

headsails: all triangular sails set ahead of the foremast

heel: to lean at an angle when sailing

hogged: said of an aging vessel whose bow and stern sag; in an extreme case, in profile, appearing to arch like a hog's back

holding ground: the harbor bottom in which a vessel is anchored

jib boom: a spar extending beyond the bowsprit

kedge: to move a vessel by laying out an anchor and hauling the vessel toward it

keel: the main structural member down the centerline of a vessel's hull. The lowest part of the hull

ketch: a two-masted vessel whose after mast is shorter than the foremast and ahead of the rudder post

knockabout rig: a vessel whose jib stay attaches at the bow with no bowsprit

knot: measure of speed; one knot is equal to 6,080.20 feet (one nautical mile, or one minute of latitude) per hour

leech: the after edge of a sail rigged fore-and-aft or the outer edge of a square sail

leeward: away from the wind

leeway: motion of a vessel to leeward, caused by the wind

lowers: the lower sails of a vessel that might have topsails

luff: n, the forward part of a sail; v, shaking of an improperly trimmed sail

marconi: a triangular sail, luff attached to the mast (as opposed to gaff-rigged)

Mayday: emergency call, SOS

on the wind: sailing as close as possible to the direction from which the wind is coming

off the wind: sailing downwind

pinky: an early, small shore-fishing schooner, distinctive for its characteristic high and narrow stern.

port: the left side of a vessel, looking forward

rake: the degree to which a mast tilts from perpendicular

reach: to sail across the wind

reef: to lessen the area of a sail, usually by tying down a portion (see photo of *Ocean Star*, page 113)

scantlings: the dimensions of a vessel's framing

schooner: vessel with two or more masts, with the after mast as tall as or taller than the other(s)

shoal-draft: a vessel that requires little depth of water to float

sheer, sheerline: the curve in the profile of the upper edge of a boat's hull

shorten sail: reef, take down sails, or replace them with smaller ones

snatch block: a block that opens so a line may be fed through it easily

square-rigged: sails rigged across the vessel, on yards centered on a mast

starboard: the right side of a vessel, looking forward

stem: the foremost upright timber of a wooden boat

stern: the after or rear section of the boat

stiff: takes a breeze without heeling to any great degree

strake: a plank or planks running the length of a vessel

transom: the athwartships, flattened part of the stern

treenail fastened: timbers and planks joined by wedged wooden pegs

trim: to adjust the sails according to wind direction

whitehall: a long, narrow, graceful rowing boat

windlass: device for bringing in the anchor chain

windward: the weather side, or side toward the wind

wing-and-wing, "wung out": with the wind coming from dead astern, sailing with at least one sail set on each side, spread like wings

yard: a horizontal spar from which a square sail is hung

yawl boat: a small powerboat that provides propulsion for a sailing vessel

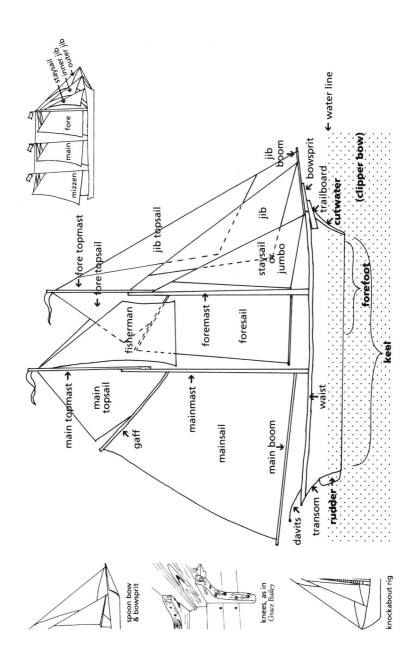

staysail
inner jib
outer jib

fore
main
mizzen

fore topmast
fore topsail
jib topsail

jib topsail

jib
boom
bowsprit
trailboard
cutwater
(clipper bow)
water line

main topmast
main topsail
gaff

fisherman

staysail
or
jumbo

jib

mainmast
foremast
foresail
mainsail
main boom
waist
davits
transom
rudder
forefoot
keel

spoon bow
& bowsprit

knees, as in
Grace Bailey

knockabout rig

Photo: Phil Roberts, Jr.

Home port for author Virginia Thorndike is Lincolnville, Maine. She and her husband both spend as much time as possible on the water, which means plenty of opportunities to sail among Penobscot Bay's windjammers and other classic sailing vessels. Photographing them naturally led her to research the vessels further, and the more she learned, she says, the more her respect for these majestic vessels grew.

Ms. Thorndike grew up in Boston and graduated from Boston University, majoring in history. Pursuing a wide variety of occupations over the years has taken her from Boston to California and back to New England. Her love of sailing reaches back to childhood summers spent on Islesboro, Maine. Sailing is in her blood; her great-grandfather was three times the Americas Cup defender, and her grandfather, a designer of sailing yachts, was also an Americas Cup contender. A former dressage and trail riding competitor, Ms. Thorndike now keeps pleasure horses (plus three dogs, eight cats, and a rooster). She is a town selectman and is active in local and regional planning in addition to pursuing her freelance writing career.